Contents

Contents (continued)

Acknowledgements

The cover illustration, taken from a publicity postcard for the Caledonian Railway for their Trossachs Tour and illustrating the first appearance of Ellen in Sir Walter Scott's *The Lady of the Lake*, appears by kind permission of the Scottish Motor Museum Trust. The map on p. 134 appears by courtesy of Ian Thompson, with cartography by Mike Shand. The Association for Scottish Literary Studies would like to thank the Loch Lomond and The Trossachs National Park for their support of the Association's successful conference in 2010, held to mark the 200th anniversary of the publication of *The Lady of the Lake*, from aspects of which this volume emerged.

Literary pilgrimage as cultural imperialism and 'Scott-land'

IAN BROWN

The publication of *The Lady of the Lake* in 1810 was, of course, a sensation. It also, as later chapters in this volume show, created – or at least reinforced, enhanced, in a modern term rebooted – a curiosity, a desire to visit the locations in which its fictional action took place. The urge to visit the Trossachs, while not originated, as we shall see, in Scott's poem, was intensified very significantly by it.

Forms of tourism linked to literature were not new. Nor were their impacts always neutral or benign. In 1759, according to Edmund Malone, the Reverend Francis Gastrell cut down a mulberry tree supposed to have been planted by Shakespeare in the grounds of New Place, his Stratford House, and razed the house itself, to 'save himself the trouble of shewing it to those whose admiration for our great poet led them to visit the poetick ground on which it stood'.[1] When Stuart Kelly says, 'What differentiates Scott's contribution to the burgeoning tourist trade is the extent to which it encompasses the author himself',[2] the point is not that Scott originated such interest in the author as focus of tourism, but the degree to which he intensified such interest. When the Grand Tour had been established over many years as educational experience, *rite de passage* and payment of homage to the cultural loci considered foundational to European culture, Walter Scott's work can hardly be said to have founded what we would now call literary, let alone cultural, tourism. Shakespeare's New Place or the sites of the Grand Tour, however, were sites where historical figures had lived. Scott tourism extended beyond his birth-town, the focus of earlier Shakespeare tourism. What is remarkable about the ways in which *The Lady of the Lake* brought tourists to the Trossachs is that they came to visit a fictional site. Or rather they came in increasing numbers to visit a pre-existing, but limited, tourist destination whose significance was much enhanced and overlaid by his creative output. Something similar could be seen in Verona where Shakespeare's fictional lovers were assigned actual locations, as in time was Scott's own Fair Maid in her spurious 'House' in Perth. Kelly notes, remarking how Scott's *Marmion* (1808) could intensify interest in even such an iconic site as that of the battle of Flodden or Scott himself in a famous beauty spot:

> Taking Morritt to see Flodden, Scott was astonished to discover at Branxton that the local pub owner wanted to rename his hostelry 'the Scott's Head' and hoped Scott would sit for a portrait. [...] Just between Melrose and Bemersyde is a lovely panorama, taking in an oxbow of the Tweed and a fine aspect of the Eildon Hills, which has become known as 'Scott's View', supposedly because the horses pulling his hearse automatically stopped there during the funeral cortege. As we have seen, after his death, Scott is over-written onto the places he described. Scott-land is a palimpsest of Scotland and Scott's works.[3]

Literary tourism reshapes its sites.

This volume explores aspects of three themes: varieties of literary tourism, the geographical, topographical and imaginary space designated 'The Trossachs', and Walter Scott's impact, particularly through his poem *The Lady of the Lake* and his novel *Rob Roy*, the former largely set in and the latter impinging on the Trossachs. The volume is organised to address all three in relationship to one another, but begins in its chapters two, three and four by considering the development of tourism in the Trossachs. In these chapters it is clear that literary tourism had an important role to play in this, but that tourism in pursuit of sport or site-seeing as 'sight-seeing' in the context of the eighteenth-century pre-Romantic cult of the sublime or picturesque both also had important roles. Meanwhile Michael Newton shows that, in this process, fundamental literary connections were neglected or even suppressed except as filtered through Macpherson's Ossianic creativity, which had its own influence on the development of Highlands tourism. The literary travellers, the Wordsworths and Coleridge – they, of course, resisted the term 'tourists' – discussed by Dorothy McMillan, first visited the area not because of Scott's writing They were in the area twice in the decade before *The Lady of the Lake* was published in search of the 'sublime' or 'picturesque', terms, however, that Dorothy Wordsworth, as McMillan makes clear, used very sparingly, even disparagingly. It is therefore important to begin any discussion of Scott's impact – or that of literary tourism in general – by careful consideration of the specific sources of tourism in the Trossachs and the genesis of the guides that promoted tourist interest.

Before doing this, one should address a range of eighteenth-century background factors that had implications for eighteenth- and nineteenth-century tourism development. One such factor, long-established, was the history of pilgrimage, going back to classical times, the visiting of sacred sites to achieve some form of enlightenment or ascribed virtue. In this context, literary, or any form of cultural, tourism can be seen to be a means of achieving either higher understandings or increased merit, something which accords with modern conceptions in tourism studies of 'authenticity' or 'endearment'. Pilgrimage can also, however, be seen as a form of cultural imperialism in that chosen sites are appropriated for value systems quite extraneous to them, which the pilgrim, or more likely the pilgrim's ideological/spiritual guru, chooses to assign to the sites. Secondly, travel can be perceived as means of education, something reflected fictively in the development in the eighteenth-century *bildungsroman*. Tobias Smollett's *The Expedition of Humphry Clinker* with its journey round Britain, including a visit to Loch Lomond so close to Smollett's birthplace in Renton, embedded in its title is an example which comes geographically particularly close to the Trossachs. The novel-as-journey-to-enlightenment is found in several of Scott's works including of course, for our purposes most aptly, *Rob Roy*. Meantime, the conception of journey-as-education, whether seen as educational method or cultural trope, is enshrined in the model of the Grand Tour. A third factor is the domestic impact of civil unrest. The failure of the 1745–46 Jacobite Rising marked a watershed in the Gàidhealtachd throughout Highlands and Islands culture and society. The specific details of that are widely discussed elsewhere, but for our purposes what can be said to matter is that, just as the 1746 Disarming Act aimed at removing the symbols of a distinctive Highland and Gaelic culture including the wearing of the kilt, playing of the Highland bagpipes and carrying of arms, so, as the Gàidhealtachd regions of Scotland were 'pacified', the development of forms of tourism were also means of developing an imperialist narrative in which native culture became exoticised rather as, in Edward Said's terminology, eastern cultures were orientalised. In this way tourism in the Highlands appropriated the Gàidhealtachd to the value systems of its new regimes. Even long-established landowners adjusted to the new political and economic structures, or, to put it another way, clan chiefs became 'improving' or exploitative landlords. Fourthly, in the post-Union settlement in Scotland, Scottish intellectuals, writers and other Enlightenment figures, led the way in imagining the idea of a united country, a 'British' nation. In this process, for example, James Thomson and David Mallet provided the lyrics and dramatic text for Thomas Arne's music in *The Masque of Alfred* (1740), which concludes with the duet between the Saxon Alfred the Great and his wife, 'Rule Britannia', in which the wonder of the new British state, here projected back in time for its foundation and seen as a single imperialist nation, are hymned. This process of britannisation of England and Scotland, a recurrent feature of eighteenth- and nineteenth- century life is largely Scottish-led, whether through the Scot John Arbuthnot's creation of John Bull in 1712 or David Hume's later attempts to expunge 'scotticisms' from his prose. One might call it 'The (Rule) Britannia Project', leading in the twentieth century to the would-be-unitary state Tom Nairn has called 'Ukania'. Fifthly, there is the regular international conflict which meant that, of the last fifty years of the eighteenth century, Britain was engaged in war with continental opponents in at least twenty-two. In those circumstances opportunities for Grand Tours were circumscribed and domestic alternatives were often sought. All of these factors created fertile grounds for the nurture of a range of tourist sites, not least by the time of the Napoleonic wars. Then, with some brief periods of truce, for twenty-three years until 1815 Britain was at war with its nearest continental mainland neighbour. And, as the conception of Britain was being developed, Scott himself, while seeking to reserve Scottish aspects to this conception, supported the idea of 'Britain'.

Alastair Durie lucidly makes the point about the interaction of the factors I have identified:

> [From the 1760s on] The British were beginning to explore the remoter parts of Britain,[4] a process periodically accelerated by war in Europe, which prevented travel there. The Grand Tour in Europe remained the first choice of higher levels of society. But what helped domestic tourism was a growing enthusiasm amongst professional and commercial society for the mini-tour, an excursion of weeks rather than months, which might be spent in France, or in the Lakes, or the North of Britain. An English lady noted in her journal of a tour from London in the summer of 1788 through Glasgow

and the Central and Northern Scotland that people were coming north at a great rate: 'all the world, it seems is travelling to Scotland or Ireland'.[5] Highland Scotland – central and western rather than the far north – was a particular beneficiary, assisted by the growing value of the Highlander in military circles and a changed perspective on the Jacobite cause, which had changed from a handicap to an asset. (p. 48)

Durie adds:

> The fact was that by the later eighteenth century Scotland – before Scott – was becoming very fashionable. Edinburgh, the Athens of the North, was already a city of culture, but it was outside the Lowlands that the growth was most remarkable. It is astonishing how quickly – in under one generation – repression after the '45 had given away to romanticisation of the Highlands. (p. 49)

One should not ascribe, then, too much influence to Scott alone. Ossian had already contributed to interest in the Highlands as a tourist destination as had such sensationalised (his)tories as that of Rob Roy. And the search for the sublime and picturesque had begun to bring tourists to the Trossachs before Scott had written his poem. But, as we shall see, Scott did bring in new tourists and also set up a virtuous circle of creativity which led from him through the work of many writers including Jules Verne and Gerard Manley Hopkins to contemporary film.

In considering the case of the Trossachs as a tourist destination against such a background, one must recognise the importance of Sir John Sinclair's *The Statistical Account of Scotland.* Tom Furniss in his chapter is very clear about this. Drawing on the work of Nicola J. Watson, he makes the point that, despite earlier tourist neglect of the area, the Trossachs were from the 1790s on, before Scott wrote *The Lady of the Lake,* already a centre of tourist interest. While he notes that

> An examination of the major published tours of and guidebooks to the Highlands of Scotland in the eighteenth century indicates that the Trossachs and Loch Katrine were almost wholly overlooked by Highland travellers until the late 1790s, (p. 31)

he observes

> Loch Katrine and the Trossachs were first brought into notice by
> the Reverend James Robertson's report on the parish of Callander
> published in 1794 in volume XI of Sinclair's *The Statistical Account of
> Scotland*. (p. 30)

One outcome of Robertson's report is that, as Furniss demonstrates,

> There is evidence to show that although Robertson's parish report
> appeared as part of the expensive multi-volume *Statistical Account
> of Scotland* and was not likely to be carried on a tour it nonetheless
> had a direct impact on some of the guidebooks written shortly after-
> wards by Scottish authors. (p. 35)

Furniss provides in his chapter detailed examples of quotation from
Robertson in several of the guidebooks produced for the area in the 1790s.
In Furniss's view, 'Robertson's parish report may be said to invent the
Trossachs' tourist and the standard itinerary'. And Furniss provides partic-
ular insight into Robertson's role in shaping the development of Trossachs
tourism within a Romantic aesthetic:

> Robertson's use of the aesthetic discourse of the Romantic tourist
> is heightened through the trope of indescribability – invoked here
> through an allusion to the claim in *Antony and Cleopatra* that
> Cleopatra's 'person/ [...] beggared all description' (II, 2, 202-3). This
> device suggests that the physical features of the Trossachs' landscape
> are too sublime to be contained by the descriptions and sketches of
> the picturesque tourist. (p. 34)

In other words, in guide-books in the later 1790s, drawing on Robertson,
sometimes verbatim, a cult of Trossachs tourism based on landscape,
sublimity and the picturesque predates – and perhaps influences – the
choice of the Trossachs as a site for the action of *The Lady of the Lake*.
Certainly Scott in visiting the Trossachs cannot but have been aware of
the framework of perception and imagination that already imbued the

landscape and topography of the Trossachs with cultural significance. That such significance existed is demonstrated not least by Dorothy Wordsworth's two visits to the area, in 1803 and 1807, discussed in Dorothy McMillan's chapter.

Before returning to the place of *The Lady of the Lake* and the Trossachs in the development of literary tourism, it is important to recognise – besides the impact of Scott and his work in general – the contextual issues to which Alastair Durie draws attention in his chapter where he considers, *inter alia*, other forms of tourism and other gateways to literary tourism like Ossian or Burns. His chapter begins:

> Between 1780 and 1830 tourism was transformed as an industry. There was a revolutionary change in scale: what had been an experience only for the elite few became an activity for every section of society by the later nineteenth century. There was a widening of direction; what had once been mainly focused on Europe became a much more diffuse stream. This was change powered by choice; more time and more free income and better transport meant more and more people could travel as they wished or were persuaded. And no destination in Europe benefited more than Scotland, a development in which Scott clearly played a very significant part. Scott's writings drew people to Scotland, and shaped where within Scotland they chose to visit. (p. 45)

Scott's role, in Durie's argument, is clear and highly influential. In effect, he transmutes the initial impact of the factors already discussed, including the aesthetic impact of the cult of the sublime and the picturesque, the 'pacification' and acculturation of the Gàidhealtachd as 'The Highlands' within the (Rule) Britannia project and the fashionability of inland tours when wars made the Grand Tour a less easy option. He observes

> The effect of his novels and poetry was in the first place general, to sell Scotland as a romantic place to discover, sufficiently different to be intriguing, distant but not dangerous, a mix of the new and the already familiar. Scotland became 'Scott-land', and Scott's land Scotland. (p. 45)

And, as Durie acutely comments,

> in all destination marketing, the dream is always worth more than
> the reality, the means less important than the end, and if the visitors
> come, then massaging is justified, truth a secondary consideration.
> (p. 46)

The point is that, in the search for the 'authentic experience', which is itself an intellectual and emotional construct, the inwards embrace of the external sight/site, the personalised emotional engagement with the tourist experience Richard Prentice has called 'endearment', there is a further transmutation akin to the spiritual impact of the focus of pilgrimage on the religious believer. Put in direct terms, as Durie observes,

> The degree of connection is seen time and again, with an example
> being that of an unknown English diarist who came to Scotland in
> successive summers. During his first short eight-day Scottish tour in
> August 1817, the recently published *Rob Roy* was clearly very much
> in his mind when he visited Glasgow. The Cathedral he describes
> as 'a place rendered immortal by being designated the Laigh Kirk in
> the novel of Rob Roy'. The following year, as part of a 'Peep at the
> Highlands', he made a point of visiting Rob Roy's celebrated cave,
> 'where it is said that Walter Scott composed part of his tale called
> Rob Roy'. (p. 47)

The transmutation, the endearment, depends at this place and time, the late 1810s and subsequent decades in Scotland, on Scott – and this was not an effect magically wrought by the 'Wizard of the North' only on Southerners. Durie observes:

> Scott did not just work his spell on English and foreign visitors, but
> on Scots who for the first time were turning their sights on their
> own country, rather than going south or to the Continent. (p. 48)

But he adds a cautionary note to any tendency the reader might have to ascribe the impacts and developments of nineteenth-century Scottish tourism simply to Scottian wizardry:

> It is tempting, because their letters and journals have survived, to assume that all tourists were on a literary and cultural tour. That is what the word tourist had meant, in Europe (cf. Pope's 'The Grand Tourist'), a particular type of traveller: 'a traveller now is called a touri-ist'.[6] But the definition was widening to take in a much wider range of travel for pleasure and leisure, those who came for sport or science, for the seaside or the hills, for education and for health. (p. 50)

As Durie emphasises, then, tourism might also arise in other important forms besides the concern of this volume, literary or cultural tourism. He reminds us, even as we focus on the latter modes, of the importance of health, sporting and landscape tourism. Nonetheless, Scott's overall impact was considerable and Durie provides a balanced judgement:

> such change in provision and improvement had to be financed, and Scott's writing was what made the tipping point, when tourism in Scotland moved from custom to commerce, from hospitality to an industry. [but ...] It would indeed simply be laziness to agree that Scott invented Scottish tourism. (p. 53)

Given this background, the question arises as to the specific impact of Scott's major Trossachs-set work, *The Lady of the Lake*, on tourism and the Trossachs. In discussing this, Nicola J. Watson, who addresses the influence specifically of the poem on tourism, makes the point that the Trossachs had a converse impact on *The Lady of the Lake*. She notes the realisation of scenery is often seen in terms of the poem, but that vice-versa:

> the poem was simplified by and for its readers, in the sense that within cultural memory there was a tendency to reduce it to the scenes set in the environs of Loch Katrine; and it was elaborated by and for readers through contemporary practices of visual depiction, performance-adaptation, and tourism itself, all of which worked to bind poem and place together within the nineteenth-century imagination. (p. 56)

In other words, while the Trossachs come in large – though not exclusive –

part to be seen through the lens of Scott's *The Lady of the Lake*, so the poem comes largely – though not exclusively – to be seen through the lens of Trossachs tourism. As Furniss has alerted us in his chapter, so Watson in hers reminds us of the impact of Scott on pre-Scott phenomena:

> Although Loch Katrine as we experience it today is very much the product of the tourism that Scott's writing inspired, the scenery of the Trossachs and the loch had been known to the local gentry as a beauty-spot since around the 1780s. The landscape was commonly described in contemporary writings in terms of a mix of the sublime (the rocky defile of the pass of the Trossachs itself and the framing heights of Ben A'an and Ben Venue) and the beautiful (the unusually deep lake and the luxuriant framing trees and ferns). The scenery at that end of the lake lent itself to being thought of in the technical terms of William Gilpin's concept of the picturesque – in terms of a repertoire of foregrounds, glimpses, prospects, side-wings, and side-screens, in short, as something to be sketched. Alexander Campbell, among others, so describes it in 1802 in his *A Journey from Edinburgh through parts of North Britain*, recommending a series of 'stations' to the would-be artist, and remarking especially on the virtues of a boat on the lake for this purpose. Dorothy Wordsworth would echo this sentiment in her account of her trip with her brother down the lake from west to east in 1803, noting that their boatman always chose the 'bonniest' part 'with greater skill than our prospect-hunters and 'picturesque travellers". (pp. 56–7)

In other words, as Watson observes, *The Lady of the Lake* 'fits into existing models of pictorial tourism, especially Canto 1'.

It is not simply in terms of pictorial tourism that *The Lady of the Lake* has meaning. Watson acutely observes that there is an underlying coding in the narrative of the poem in which leading characters can be seen, within its political themes and historical background, to pre-shadow the later cults of leisure tourism, 'getting away from it all':

> [Fitz-James] is the king indulging himself in the pleasures of travelling incognito, pleasing himself with pretending to be a landless knight, a huntsman escaping to a land of Spenserian romance,

indulging himself therefore in something very much like a tourist fantasy. His encounter with the Trossachs and its inhabitants involves a sentimental susceptibility to the charms of the lady of the lake and her island retreat. If Fitz-James seems like a variant of the tourist, the incognito exiled Douglas household romantically living rough effectively model the ideal holiday escape from the everyday. Ellen presides over the perfect accommodation for the incognito king, embodying a sense that it is possible to escape everyday duties and responsibilities to somewhere secret, romantic, alternative, and temporary, a holiday house in which one's normal social identity can be cast aside, without forfeiting one's class privileges. [...] The poem thus models the tourist's relation to the landscape – attraction, flirtation, followed by a wistfully regretful romantic distance and discreet management of responsibility; as such, it is a real holiday romance. (pp. 59–60)

The Lady of the Lake, at one level, can be read as an escape to Renaissance-set romance and an invitation to the reader to explore the physical context that in imagination accommodated its action. It can also be read, Watson suggests, as itself embodying a proto-tourist experience, certainly for the sporting-tourist king, who hunts incognito. Perhaps less securely, though still persuasively, she argues for the political exiles who create for a time a sanctuary in an alternative world as proto-tourists. For the latter, however, one must observe that 'tourism' is also enforced internal exile.

Scott's awareness of the transmuting context of his poem is surely quite explicit. As Watson notes 'Scott embroiders the verse narrative with a mass of antiquarian footnotes drawn from contemporary guidebooks and topographical writings' (p. 60). As readers, we become, through Scott's antiquarianism, tourists-in-time, but we are also landscape-tourists informed by guidebooks drawn on by Scott and on which, as Furniss reminds us, Robertson and his contribution to *The Statistical Account* were highly influential. Scott is producing an artefact in *The Lady of the Lake* in which his notes are clearly part of the literary mise-en-scène. One is reminded of the stage directions later included by Bernard Shaw and J. M. Barrie in the published texts of their plays. With these they sought to provide their readers' minds' eyes with, often witty, reportage of the original production choices, so seeking to make their published plays not simply script, but an intermediate experience between the script read in the study and the play performed. As Watson observes, Martin Meisel, the great drama (and Shavian) scholar clearly makes the general point about Scott's impact in 'staging' *The Lady of the Lake* and 'staging' the Trossachs in his poem:

> This literary tourist impulse can be related to something more nebulous and widespread, what Martin Meisel identifies as the twinned contemporary impulses towards 'realisation' and 'illustration' of texts characteristic of nineteenth-century culture.[7] The first, as described by Meisel, is a desire to 'materialise' the text in physical form; the second is a desire to extend and elaborate the text's own sense of itself, through providing additional material in the shape of further information both textual and visual. In practice, these two impulses defined and supported one another, as can be seen in the many adaptations of *The Lady of the Lake* for both public and private performance (in the forms of parlour music, private theatricals, civic cantatas, stage melodrama, and grand opera) and the extensive industry in 'illustrating' the poem, visualising its narrative and its setting and amplifying its antiquarian materials. Arguably, the practice of literary tourism to Loch Katrine was effectively simply a variant of the widespread contemporary practices of illustrating and adapting *The Lady of the Lake*; but equally it seems likely that it was fuelled by them. (pp. 60–1)

It is precisely the theatricality of the richness of Scott's mise-en-scènes, not only in *The Lady of the Lake*, but in his other work, that makes him in the view of Martin Esslin, as expressed to the present author, the greatest artist in any art form in the nineteenth century. The richness of these mise-en-scènes allowed the multitude of adaptations and derivatives in a variety of artforms, not least, in significance for Scotland, the nineteenth-century National Drama discussed by Barbara Bell.[8]

By way of illustration of Scott's influence, Watson draws attention to the impact of *The Lady of the Lake* on the French-American travel-writer Louis Simond's experience of visiting Loch Katrine:

> Simond's account is threaded throughout with quotation from the poem, which has the double effect of giving Scott's topographical

descriptions of the place documentary credibility and inlaying the place with the scenes of romance. [...] tourists integrated their experience of the poem with the landscape. Some had it by heart and recited it for the benefit of fellow tourists; some had brought a copy borrowed from the piles thoughtfully provided at the hotel; some had merely brought a guidebook with the relevant stanzas extracted; some plotted the action on a map; some had it recited to them by the boatmen or guides.[9] Simond's sense of having the scene before him is reiterated over and over again as tourists enhanced the landscape by 'seeing' figures ambiguously remembered or imagined from the poem. (pp. 64–5)

And Scott's impact became wider and continues to this day:

As the names of two of these steamers [on Loch Katrine – *Rob Roy* and *Sir Walter Scott*] suggest, the longevity of literary tourism to Loch Katrine owed something to the ways in which Scott had subsequently populated the larger area with other characters and incidents featured in the Waverley novels. *The Lady of the Lake* was overlaid and supplemented by cultural memory of, in particular, *Waverley* (1814), *Old Mortality* (1816), and *Rob Roy* (1817). This produced a set of possible literary destinations and excursions increasingly linked through the concept of 'Scott country'. A tourist coming from the direction of Glasgow might start by visiting those sites in Glasgow associated with *Rob Roy*, such as the crypt of the cathedral, turn aside to examine others in Aberfoyle (notably the Bailie Nicol Jarvie inn and Jean McAlpine's inn), and, in travelling along Loch Ard, note the cliffs from which Helen MacGregor caused the unfortunate Morris to be thrown. (p. 66)

The impact continues, if somewhat muted. The *Sir Walter Scott* was launched on 31 October, 1899 and still runs on the loch, Scott's 'Lake', today. Meantime, however much his continuing influence has faded into the background of the popular consciousness, it can still have an impact. In 2010 the Association for Scottish Literary Studies published a bicentenary edition of *The Lady of the Lake*. Copies have sold well from the tourist shop at Loch Katrine.

Notwithstanding such a recent surge of interest, it may be argued that at times in the last century Scott's explicit impact on Trossachs tourism has persisted only in the naming of a boat. But of course his continuing implicit impact is seen in underlying ways, like changed topographical names: Ellen's Isle is a locus renamed through the influence of *The Lady of the Lake*. What we are arguing here and what chapters two to four make clear is that, while Scott is not alone in modifying, changing, developing and overlaying ways of seeing and understanding the Trossachs and, indeed, a wide range of other Scottish – and even in a case like Kenilworth English – loci, his impact is highly significant. Yet, while recognising Scott's prominent, even leading, role, in influencing perceptions of the Trossachs, the Highlands and Scotland, we should also, in considering Scott's role in literary approaches to the Trossachs, recognise the wide range of writers and artists who have engaged with the area, some of course, themselves influenced by Scott. Important, then, as the imbrication of Scott's work with the Trossachs is – a matter we will return to – Jim Alison's chapter reminds us of the wider range of anglophone literary engagements with the Trossachs. And, as Alison's and Michael Newton's chapters remind us, many artists' interactions with the area arise before Scott's writing and extend beyond the anglophone or simply literary. Writers' links with the Trossachs, as Newton makes evident, of course, predated Scott: a substantial, and much earlier, Gaelic literature related to the area. So, although some writers were influenced by Scott, he was by no means an exclusive influence. Nevertheless, Alison does identify ways in which Scott accentuates aspects of the Trossachs and so conditions contemporary perceptions of the area and its people. The ways we comprehend the Trossachs over the last two hundred years have been implicitly and inescapably affected by Scott's writing.

Alison illustrates his point with a discussion of passages from Scott novels, beginning with *Rob Roy*:

> In one memorable exchange with Nicol Jarvie, the Glasgow merchant, Helen MacGregor describes herself as an impetuous natural force like a Highland torrent; and later the MacGregors stage a clan gathering in the amphitheatre of a cataract which is meant to impress the Sassenach. This fall at Ledard, which Scott had himself visited, features in two of his novels. In *Waverley* the *picturesque*, feminine

> aspect of the three-stage cascade is emphasised, its surrounds having
> been planted out by Flora MacIvor with shrubs that 'added to the
> grace without diminishing the romantic wildness of the scene'. (p. 75)

As Alison makes clear, Scott's ascription of 'grace' and 'romantic wildness',
while still impinging on modern perceptions of the area were, even as
they developed, capable of subversion by other versions of 'reality' or
'authenticity':

> Cockburn also knew from firsthand experience that Scott's repre-
> sentations had created a beguiling Trossachs of the mind far from
> the landscape and experiences that travellers would encounter on the
> ground. (p. 76)

However the dynamic developed between objective and subjective and
between topography and tourist, cultural tourism post-Scott brought an
important and influential body of artists in to the area from many parts
of the world. Alison mentions in particular the complex interactions of
Ruskin, his wife Effie and Millais, overseas visitors like Krystyn Lach-
Szyrma or Theodor Fontane, painters like the Glasgow Boys and poets like
Gerard Manley Hopkins.

Before considering the important issues Michael Newton raises about
the importance of the original Gaelic culture in the area, it is helpful to
consider a number of points David Hewitt raises about forces that had come
to play in the area by the time Scott was writing. Hewitt's chapter discusses
the ways in which *Rob Roy* sets categories through which we are induced
to consider the nature of Highland society by the time Scott is writing his
poem. In doing do, he identifies social and economic forces which came
to bear in the eighteenth century on Highland society and its economy.
Those forces are embodied in two travellers – rather than tourists – whose
journeys through the novel bring them into contact and conflict with
Highland traditions through their own differing assumptions and priori-
ties. In turn they embody eighteenth-century economic and social ideas in
which, in fictional terms, they are ahead of their time (1715), although as
Hewitt reminds us, the novel is framed as a recollection of its events from
much later in the century, 1763:

> They [Osbaldistone and Jarvie] are both practical businessmen, and within the novel they also articulate an ideology of economic development. The notes in the Edinburgh edition show that they appear to quote eighteenth-century works on business and economics such as Bernard de Mandeville's *The Fable of the Bees*, Adam Smith's *The Wealth of Nations*, Malachy Postlethwayt's *Universal Dictionary of Trade and Commerce*, Daniel Defoe's *A Tour Through the Whole Island of Great Britain*, and Thomas Pennant's *A Tour in Scotland and Voyage to the Hebrides MDCCLXXII*. Of course they are not meant to be quoting these works, every one of which was published after 1715, but giving them words from such works makes them the articulators not just of the literature but the eighteenth-century ideology of improvement via business and commerce. (p. 90)

The ideology, especially as represented by Jarvie, however jovial and common-sense his character may at times seem, is seen as potent, but brutal and, so, in human terms, limited and limiting, As Hewitt observes

> Jarvie has written off half the population of the Highlands as lazy, under-employed, dishonest, disorderly and violent. It is genocide, not in fact but in attitude; it is the kind of nation-killing to which Sir Thomas Browne objects in *Religio Medici*. It may seem extreme to draw this conclusion from the words of a wonderfully comic character who provides a superbly comic version of 'An Inquiry into the Causes which facilitate the Rise and Progress of Rebellions and Insurrections in the Highlands of Scotland, &c', which was a 1747 analysis of the causes of the '45, possibly written by Robert Graham of Gartmore. But Frank objects, asking "'is it possible [...] that this can be a just picture of so large a portion of the island of Great Britain'" (209). And the Baillie's argument is so theoretical, so extreme, so committed to a general conclusion and so unadmitting of any variation or complexity, that any thinking person will not take his conclusions seriously. He describes a model which our general experience of human nature must lead us to reject. (p. 92)

Yet, as Scott wrote, the Clearances were under way. Hewitt is clear that, whatever his political stance might be, Scott the artist embodies the counterpoint to the economic determinism of the 'improver' when he observes 'what we are told by Diana Vernon and Rob Roy shows that the mercantile expansionism of the business community had real costs and created real pain' (p. 93).

The more distant fictional past of *The Lady of the Lake* allows the development and consolidation of romantic Trossachs tourism post-Scott with an emphasis on landscape, the sublime and the picturesque, but *Rob Roy*, published only seven years later and dealing with events by then only a century old and still politically sensitive, offers a counter-view, one which still offers the 'grace' and 'romantic wildness' seen in Waverley, but also identifies the area as the site of oppression. As Hewitt puts it,

> the Osbaldistones of Northumberland and the MacGregors of the Trossachs are victims of state oppression. They live at the margins, but they have also been forcibly marginalised, turned into victims by the laws which enforce the rule and mercantile ideology of the Hanoverian state. (p. 95)

Hewitt goes on to observe, 'In *Rob Roy* the political and economic forces which pressurise the marginalised in Northumberland and the Highlands are exercised through laws and the legal system'. He reminds us too that, as the novel reflects on its action from the perspective of half a century, it does not convey any Panglossian sentiments: Frank Osbaldistone's rumination is not on entirely positive themes. As Hewitt says,

> He married Die Vernon and in so doing he symbolically united traditions; but he has lost her; similarly the old-fashioned ways of the people of Northumberland and the Trossachs have been destroyed by modernity.
> [...]
> Thus *Rob Roy* is not just a Hanoverian novel. It is also an imperial novel. It is a novel which tangentially raises questions about the morality of imperial rule, and about the inevitable oppression of indigenous peoples in the interests of trade, and in the name of freedom.
> [...]

> Frank Osbaldistone, writing in 1763, is deeply melancholic, and is
> exacerbating his misery by going over the train of events by which he
> won his beloved wife. He is also a cultural historian shocked at the
> destruction of 'native' cultures, a destruction in which he as owner
> of Osbaldistone Hall has participated. (pp. 96–7)

The importance of the 'native' culture of the Trossachs is a key theme
of Michael Newton's chapter. This, in a timely and significant intervention,
reminds us of the ancient literary traditions of the region chiefly in Gaelic.
Despite Scott's rhetorical address,

> Harp of the North! that mouldering long hast hung
> On the witch-elm that shades Saint Fillan's spring [...],

Newton observes that the Trossachs and surrounding areas, essentially
the ancient regions of the Lennox and the Menteith, were rich in a
history of literary production. This is fully aware of the stimulus of the
landscape, topography and flora and fauna in the way that *The Lady of the
Lake* embodies. More, as Newton sharply comments, that tradition lived
contemporaneously with the writing of *The Lady of the Lake*. This is not
the place for a disquisition on linguistic imperialism in the Highlands, but
there can be no doubt that, simultaneously with the continuing attempts
to suppress Gaelic and consequently its literature, Scott and those he influenced were in turn influenced by the Gaelic traditions not least as filtered to
a Scottish anglophone community through the works of James Macpherson
as he produced his Ossianic texts. In Gaelic literature a high importance is
placed on the immanence of place and Ossian flows out of a shared Gaelic
tradition which in its transmuted Macphersonian form brought tourists to
the Trossachs before *The Lady of the Lake*, visitors whose attendance Scott's
poem increased, but did not originate. And while Scott was writing such
novels as *Rob Roy* there was a living tradition of writing which included the
Gaelic elegy for Rob Roy cited by Newton, which is different in perspective
from that of Scott and his followers, but certainly, well into the nineteenth
century, lives strongly and creatively.

In fact Scott could not have been entirely oblivious to the living
tradition in Gaelic of the time. After all, the language was to be heard
spoken all around the area. But he stood outside that language community

and the versions of its literature available to him were in a sense anglicised, exoticised – even 'orientalised' – and at a remove from the living contemporary Gaelic tradition. And Newton makes the piquant point that, since a number of the Gaelic bards of the time were trilingual, it is more than probable that there was a reverse influence back from Scott into nineteenth-century Gaelic poetry. He observes of *The Lady of the Lake*:

> The poem is meant as a compliment to the people of Loch Katrine-side, who must have been able to understand his message. To be sure, Gaelic was still spoken by many of what population was left into the early twentieth century. It is surely worth considering the suggestion,[10] even though insufficient information survives to evaluate it, that Donnchadh is asserting the primacy of this location in direct response to the local competing claims resulting from the imaginative and tourist-oriented literature and entrepreneurial tourism, explored in detail in the other chapters in this volume. (p. 107)

However that may be, Newton's penultimate paragraph summarises and tellingly anathematises a misconception embedded in *The Lady of the Lake*:

> The literary conceit in the 'Lady of the Lake' that the native minstrel harp of the Highlands generally or of the Trossachs specifically had fallen asleep until he aroused it is clearly fraudulent. Native Gaels were still actively engaged in their own literary tradition when Scott's poem was published and long afterwards. However we may judge the literature of Scott, whether according to the standards of English literature of his times or of our own, what is galling is that it is this literature that has come to represent the Trossachs to the exclusion of that composed in Gaelic by the natives themselves over many centuries. (p. 111)

Literary tourists were surely deaf and blind to that literature. 'Improvement' had a leading role in accelerating a process of post-1746 anglophonic colonialism and a commensurate downgrading of respect for Gaelic poetry under way since James VI's 1609 Statutes of Iona with their proscription of 'bards'. This led to a sometimes strange interaction between the native tradition which Hewitt has described as suffering 'destruction' and the literary tourist, or – as Dorothy McMillan's chapter suggests the Wordsworths would prefer the terminology – visitors. When William Wordsworth comes across a living example of the contemporary native Gaelic literary tradition we find it transmuted into 'The Solitary Reaper', a great poem, of course, but a baffled one as it concludes:

> Whate'er the theme, the Maiden sang
> As if her song could have no ending;
> I saw her singing at her work,
> And o'er the sickle bending;–
> I listen'd, motionless and still;
> And, as I mounted up the hill,
> The music in my heart I bore,
> Long after it was heard no more.

Wordsworth might have heard the sound of the music and held it 'in my heart', but his mind has no access to the meaning of the words of the song.

Such ignorance was part of a wider problem, one which has had a continuing impact and modern implications. Newton observes

> The trenchant anti-Ossianic camp reinforced negative attitudes about Gaelic literary tradition and many refused to acknowledge that it had one. These prejudices have continued to sour perceptions in many quarters to the present. While Gaelic literature has had a very different trajectory of development from English literature, and operates according to a different set of parameters, it deserves to be recognised as legitimate in its own right and on its own terms.[11] The anglophone tradition has deeply colonised the Highland landscape and the metaphorical literary landscape, and the post-colonial project of recognising, reclaiming, and revitalising Gaelic tradition has barely begun. It is particularly through this medium that the people of this region expressed their hopes, fears, delights, and desires. Their voices have a right to be heard and their literature deserves to be rediscovered. (p. 111)

Certainly such a progressive perception as this was not to be found in literary tourists who visited the Trossachs in the early nineteenth century.

Among the most famous of the literary travellers to the Trossachs in the decade before *The Lady of the Lake* was published must surely be William and Dorothy Wordsworth. In understanding the interactions of literary tourism, the Trossachs and Walter Scott, it is valuable to consider their visits (and their later reflections on them) for what they reveal about their attitudes not just to the area and its attractions, but also to tourism itself as a phenomenon. As Dorothy McMillan comments,

> the notion of Dorothy as a kind of tour-guide whose main function was to point out the sights to the tourist William, and subsequently to write about them, to fix their experiences for the future, is not one that would have appealed much to either of them. Like some before them and like many after them, the Wordsworths did not quite see themselves as tourists: tourists, as we know, are always other people.
>
> Nor did the Wordsworths have a very high opinion of tourist literature; like their friend Stoddart before them, they tended to disparage the genre to which they were contributing. '*Tours*,' says John Stoddart in his Preface to his *Remarks on Local Scenery and Manners in Scotland*, 'are the mushroom produce of every summer, and Scotland has had her share'.[12] (p. 114–5)

McMillan argues that a key concept in later theories of tourism and its motivations lie at the root of Dorothy's attitude. For her, McMillan argues, travelling and tourism are differentiated by the quality of the traveller's or tourist's response:

> Central to her feelings about description is the sense that the authentic experience is an imaginative and poetic one. Experience of the physical world, natural and human, may, indeed must, feed the poet but the writing of descriptive tours for their own sake is a relatively lowly activity, an act of friendship, perhaps, but not a self-authenticating act nor one which provides anything as significant as poetry. (p. 115)

In this is embedded a hierarchy of response: the 'authentic' is the poetic, while descriptive writing is 'not a self-authenticating act'. Yet one would now argue that the tourist/pilgrim seeks an 'authentic' – even 'self-authenticating' – experience. The Wordsworths' visit as considered by Dorothy is more than she herself perhaps recognised. McMillan observes

> But in spite of Dorothy's protestations the *Recollections* are travel writing of a high, if unconventional, kind. They achieve her declared aim to make her readers feel that they have been there, and that they understand how specific places affected their friends, William and Dorothy Wordsworth and briefly Coleridge too; that, in short, they have shared an experience of these places as they were at a particular moment. And because they are addressed to friends, the self that composes and the selves that are revealed are peculiarly important. These selves, these friends of the readers, can be understood through the effects of place on their imaginations. Yet, this brings another series of problems – it is not merely that the failure to take notes may damage accuracy, but that the very process of writing down may be denaturing. (p. 116)

This process of 'denaturing' is, at its most extreme, what I would call 'pilgrimage imperialism' and its cultural impact in neglecting indigenous culture is well exposed by Michael Newton in his chapter.

McMillan perceptively discusses, in the case of Dorothy Wordsworth, the intellectual and emotional processes undergone.

> The movement of the mind displaces the physical scenery into a mental landscape, yet also links the natural to romance literary tradition and popular entertainment: it is a democratic mode of perception, and a poetic one, and one that importantly begins and ends in sociability. (p. 118)

These are not, in this interpretation, simply negative processes. They are complex and can be seen to have positive outcomes, though with a price paid. And yet it is not simply a case of the traveller's or tourist's denaturing the object of gaze nor expropriating other cultures. The other has her or his own mental landscape. Dorothy Wordsworth, quoted by McMillan, observes that he who transports her and her brother

'is attached to the lake by some sentiment of pride, as his own
domain' and has a rare sense of what is fitting behaviour to the travellers in his own home: he is courteous and attentive without servility,
and his sense of how memory and retelling are part of travel is joyful
and sensitive, as he repeats 'from time to time that we should often
tell of this night when we got to our own homes' (1, 277). (p. 119)

It may be argued that Dorothy Wordsworth is hardly a dispassionate
witness in her own case, but, unless we are to accuse her of bad faith,
it is possible to see in her report of the boatman's 'pride' in 'his own
domain' his culture and its own perceptions of nature the kind of still-
prevailing Gaelic culture discussed in Michael Newton's chapter. What
is more, there is a clear hint of an oral story-telling tradition in his
reference to 'tell[ing] of this night'. And the re-iteration of the experience in retelling embeds the physical experience in, in McMillan's words,
'a mental landscape'.

McMillan, further, reinforces the point Michael Newton makes – one to
which I have already referred – about visitors' ignorance about and neglect
of the indigenous, ancient literature of the region:

> Some of William's most famous poems had their source in the two
> visits to the Trossachs: 'The Highland Girl', 'Stepping Westward' and
> 'The Solitary Reaper'. In all three the imaginative experience depends
> on mysteries not being cleared up. But Dorothy Wordsworth's object
> is generally to remove mystery, to give more and more information
> until the people she meets, men and women, acquire a life indepen-
> dent of her own imaginings. (p. 120)

However Dorothy sets out to unravel it, the mystery lies in substantial
part in the language of the community travelled through. In William's
unknowing poetic response to 'The Solitary Reaper' referred to earlier, a
response Dorothy Wordsworth would call 'authentic' as being 'imaginative
and poetic', he actually creates inauthenticity, because he cannot approach
the reality of the reaper's expression or experience. Yet, in Dorothy's travel
writing, she approaches greater 'authenticity', not as a literary artefact, but
in seeking as truthful a report as she can. Such 'authentic' experience of the

place and people is a touristic objective, however often compromised by cultural distance or commercial exploitation.

Nothing is simple when one seeks 'authenticity'. Dorothy Wordsworth's disparaging of tourists guides is rendered a little ironic when McMillan notes the impact of her travel writing:

> And, of course, Dorothy's account went with William and Mary when they toured with Sara Hutchison in 1814. Sara showed an interest in the people she encountered that was possibly stimulated by her reading of Dorothy's recollections. In her journal Sara writes of a household in the Trossachs: 'The man sat making a rake and conversed sensibly upon all subjects – he had an excellent library in the *spence* – many new books such as Mrs Grant on the Highlands, Scott's poems and many county histories – besides some old books of value'.[13] (p. 121)

Indeed, as McMillan shows, Dorothy Wordsworth's own trajectory highlights the change in perceptions of – and motivations for – visiting the Trossachs. And Sara Hutchison's observation of how Walter Scott's poetic vision is embraced in the country craftsman's spence adds another layer of irony and complexity. Indeed, as McMillan comments, these layers of complexity are part of a wider transformative process with regard not only to visions of the Trossachs, but of Scotland in general:

> And so, the generic change in Dorothy Wordsworth's writing is intimately bound up with a change in Scotland and the Highlands of Scotland in particular, a change wrought at least in part by the transformation of the Trossachs after *The Lady of the Lake*. Before 1810 there were those 'inhabited solitudes' which Dorothy Wordsworth so brilliantly celebrates as she characterises both the land and its inhabitants and these 'inhabited solitudes' were fit for poetry and for a prose, like Dorothy's, that filled the necessary silences of poetry, thus providing a kind of broad hinterland for poetry. After 1810 the Highlands had become a land fit for the nineteenth century novel with all that novel's clash and intermingling of culture and opinion. It is perhaps a pity that Dorothy Wordsworth never wrote such a novel, but it is not a pity that she was unable to shape, or deform, her *Recollections* into tourist fodder. (p. 122)

Out of all this complexity, one thing is clear: while Dorothy Wordsworth never wrote that novel, subsequent artists were stimulated by the ironies and complexities of Scott and post-Scott visions of the Trossachs and of Scotland to write novels and poetry, to paint and to make films.

The remaining chapters of this volume each develop specific artform aspects of its themes. Murdo Macdonald's chapter reinforces from the perspective of the visual arts many of the points made by earlier chapters, demonstrating the ways in which visual responses to Macpherson and Ossian, and to Burns, predated Scott. In turn, Scott's writing, no doubt affected by their pictorial influences, reinforced and profoundly modified them. He also makes clear the ways in which Scott stimulated a number of important nineteenth-century visual artists, not least J. M. W. Turner, who worked directly from Scott's works in preparing images of the Highlands which were themselves important in shaping the public's perceptions of that landscape. While he notes the conventional impact of Landseer's images of the Highlands, he contrasts the far richer and deeper impact of Scott's influence on visual artists.

Ian Thompson meanwhile, in discussing Jules Verne's Scottish novels, offers what is in effect a case study of the impact of Scott on a later nineteenth-century novelist, one whose nationality reinforces Martin Esslin's assessment of the international significance of Scott's influence. As Thompson notes, Verne, who claimed descent on his mother's side from a Scottish archer in the service of King Louis XI of France, 'was a passionate admirer of Sir Walter Scott'. In an interview with a journalist in 1895 he enthused about 'beautiful picturesque Edinburgh, with its Heart of Midlothian, and many entrancing memories; the Highlands, world-forgotten Iona, and the wild Hebrides', continuing 'Of course, to one familiar with the works of Scott, there is scarce a district of his native land lacking some association connected with the writer and his immortal work'.[14] Thompson discusses in detail several works by Verne with Scottish – and Scott-influenced – connections, pointing out, for example, that in each of the Scottish novels we find

> a romantic heroine, portrayed in the most favourable light, and in three cases given a name close to Ellen. In *The Children of Captain Grant*, Lord Glenarvan's wife is Lady Helena. In *The Green Ray*, the heroine is Helena Campbell, and in *The Underground City*, the 'Child of the Cavern' is called Nell, a diminutive form of 'Helen'. (p. 139)

Above all, Thompson discusses *The Underground City*, set in and under the Trossachs, describing it as embodying 'Verne's admiration for Sir Walter Scott and his own distant Scottish roots', and the Trossachs as stimulating his 'creative imagination' and resulting in 'his most successful Scottish novel'.

Finally, David Manderson's chapter considers the history of film in the Trossachs. He also demonstrates with considerable detail the many ways in which the Trossachs, or sites intended to be the Trossachs, have been employed in a wide variety of screen manifestations whether in film or television. As he shows, Scott provided a central starting point for the depiction of Scotland on the screen, alongside, as Richard Butt has identified, two others of a founding triumvirate, Robert Louis Stevenson and J. M. Barrie.[15] His influence, however, extends far beyond screen versions of his own work, like the several versions of *Rob Roy*, whether to the actual sites selected for location shots for A. J. Cronin's Dr Finlay as televised in the influential BBC series or the setting for the film *Geordie*, an archetypical example of a certain kind of self-ironising and whimsical Highland *jeu d'esprit*. In all of this, Manderson observes 'the Trossachs can claim to be a major centre of film production. The list of films or television programmes which either feature it strongly as a location or use it as a single location among many others, is impressive'. While, as he notes, 'we should bear in mind that screen dramas distort real locations more than literary texts, using them for their own ends and choosing how much to reinvent them', he concludes by reminding us

> the Trossachs became embedded in popular consciousness as the very embodiment of Scottish Romanticism through the work of Scott. As a tourist area, it was already well known to filmmakers when film was young, or to location scouts if they wanted to set a film here. Through Scott's work people already knew of the magic of this borderland between Highland and Lowland, old religion and new, English and Gaelic, Protestant and Catholic, and they knew of its scenery. It was ready-made to be transferred into a visual medium. And that type of visual storytelling was forming the way people read and saw the world long before films came along. (p. 151)

Indeed Manderson concludes his chapter with a striking passage from *Rob Roy* in which he shows how Scott's visualising imagination, whether in poetry or novel, was what we would now call 'filmic'.

This volume, then, demonstrates, from a wide variety of complementary perspectives, that in a panoply of writers and artists who have developed modern perceptions of Scotland, the Highlands and, specifically, the Trossachs, Scott led in developing a whole new strand of seeing the landscape, Scotland and its culture. In so doing, he also invented a whole new strand of literary tourism. However the modern might wish to interrogate aspects of Scott's imagined worlds, he has undoubtedly shaped the very ways in which, not just through his writing, but in everyday life, we see the sites/sights about which he wrote. Scott's powerful reconceptions and imaginative explorations of human nature and its societies continue to affect, even if sometimes now only implicitly, our ways of seeing. And, within that larger legacy, the Trossachs continue to be constantly revisited and reimagined in the light of Scott's creative mind.

Notes

1 *The Plays and Poems of Shakespeare* (London: Bohn, 1853) Vol. II, p. 118, fn. 6. I am grateful to Professor J. R. Mulryne for assisting me in tracing this reference.
2 Stuart Kelly, *Scott-land: The Man Who Invented A Nation* (Edinburgh: Polygon, 2010), p. 97
3 Ibid.
4 Malcolm Andrews, *The Search for the Picturesque, Landscape, Aesthetics and Tourism in Britain, 1760–1800* (Aldershot: Scolar Press, 1989), chapter 8, pp. 197–240: 'The Highlands Tour and the Ossianic Sublime.'
5 Glasgow University Library, Special Collections MS Gen. 738: Mrs Diggle, *Journal of a tour from London to the Highlands of Scotland*, 19 April to 7 August 1788, Letter 23rd, Gretna.
6 Samuel Pegge, *Anecdotes of the English Language*, (1800) cited in the *Oxford English Dictionary*.
7 Martin Meisel, *Realizations: Narrative, Pictorial, and Theatrical Arts in Nineteenth-century England* (Princeton: Princeton University Press, 1983), p. 30.
8 Barbara Bell, 'The National Drama, Joanna Baillie and the National Theatre', in Ian Brown *et al.* (eds.) *The Edinburgh History of Scottish Literature* (Edinburgh: Edinburgh University Press, 2007) vol. 2, pp. 228–35, and 'The National Drama and the Nineteenth Century', in Ian Brown (ed.), *The Edinburgh Companion to Scottish Drama* (Edinburgh: Edinburgh University Press, 2011), pp. 47–59.
9 For further details, see Nicola J. Watson, *The Literary Tourist: Readers and Places in Romantic and Victorian Britain* (Basingstoke: Palgrave Macmillan, 2006), pp. 160–2.
10 Made to Michael Newton by Tom Furniss during the discussion at the ASLS conference, 'Scott, the Trossachs and the Tourists', Balloch, 5–6 June 2010.
11 William Gillies, 'On the Study of Gaelic Literature', in *Litreachas & Eachdraidh: Rannsachadh na Gàidhlig 2, Glaschu 2002 / Literature & History: Papers from the Second Conference of Scottish Gaelic Studies, Glasgow 2002*, ed. by Michel Byrne, Thomas Owen Clancy & Sheila Kidd (Glasgow: University of Glasgow, 2006), pp. 1–32.
12 John Stoddart, *Remarks on Local Scenery and Manners in Scotland during the Years 1799 and 1800*, 2 vols (London: W. Miller, 1801), vol. 1, p. viii.

13 Quoted in Mary Moorman, *William Wordsworth: A Biography; the Later Years, 1803–1850* (Oxford: Clarendon Press, 1965), p. 259, note.
14 M Belloc, 'Jules Verne at Home', *Strand Magazine*, February, 1895.
15 Richard Butt, 'Literature and the Screen Media since 1908' in Ian Brown *et al.* (ed.) *The Edinburgh History of Scottish Literature* (Edinburgh: Edinburgh University Press, 2007), vol. 3, pp. 53–63.

'A place much celebrated in England': Loch Katrine and the Trossachs before *The Lady of the Lake*

TOM FURNISS

If we are to assess the role of Sir Walter Scott's *The Lady of the Lake* (1810) in making the Trossachs and Loch Katrine into one of the most magnetic Romantic localities in Scotland we need to bear in mind that it was Loch Lomond that attracted travellers and tourists in the eighteenth century, not Loch Katrine, and that the impact of Scott's poem in alluring large numbers of visitors to the Trossachs was resented by those who made a living out of tourism to Loch Lomond and its surrounding landscape.[1] John Campbell Shairp included the following anecdote in an endnote to his edition of Dorothy Wordsworth's *Recollections of a Tour Made in Scotland, AD 1803* (first published in 1874):

> when [Robert] Jamieson, the editor of the fifth edition of [Edmund] Burt's *Letters [from a Gentleman in the North of Scotland]*, was in the Highlands in 1814, [...] he met a savage-looking fellow on the top of Ben Lomond, [...] who told him that he had been a guide to the mountain for more than forty years, but now 'a Walter Scott' had spoiled his trade. 'I wish,' said he, 'I had him a ferry over Loch Lomond; I should be after sinking the boat, if I drowned myself into the bargain, for ever since he wrote his "Lady of the Lake," as they call it, everybody goes to see that filthy hole, Loch Ketterine. The devil confound his ladies and his lakes!'[2]

We also need to remember that Scott was not the pioneer of tourism to Loch Katrine and the Trossachs. Nicola Watson claims that when Scott first visited the Trossachs in the summer of 1809 he was following 'a well-defined tourist route and itinerary', and that 'In choosing the Trossachs as the setting for *The Lady of the Lake*, Scott had in fact pitched upon an area already sufficiently famous for the type of sublime and picturesque scenery beloved of hunters after landscape thrills.'[3] A letter from Sir John Sinclair to Scott, dated 6 November 1810, indicates that tourists were already visiting

Loch Katrine before the publication of *The Lady of the Lake* and that Scott's poem gave a huge boost to such tourism:

> I was fortunate enough to have a very favourable day for visiting the beauties of Loch Catharine, in the fame of which I take a peculiar interest, as it was first brought into notice by the Publication of the Statistical Account of Scotland. [...] You have increased the number of visitors to Loch Catharine *beyond measure*; my carriage was the 297th in the course of this year, and there never had been above 100 before in any one season when its fame rested solely on prosaic eulogiums.[4]

Sinclair's letter also supports one of the central claims of the present chapter – that Loch Katrine and the Trossachs were first brought into notice by the Reverend James Robertson's report on the parish of Callander published in 1794 in volume XI of Sinclair's *The Statistical Account of Scotland*.[5]

Yet although the Trossachs and Loch Katrine may have already been sufficiently famous when Scott visited them in 1809, it seems unlikely that they were visited by a hundred carriages in any year during the 1790s. Alastair J. Durie reminds us that Highland travellers in the 1790s were few and far between:

> [T. C.] Smout guesses that, at the turn of the century, the Highlands were seeing at best a few hundred visitors annually, although this was an increase on the numbers thirty years previously. Travellers' accounts tend to confirm this picture of a region penetrated only by a handful. [...] [Malcolm] Andrews points out that Dr Garnet [*sic*] met not a single other traveller during the first three weeks of his tour in the Highlands during July 1798, though this was the height of the travelling season.[6]

Furthermore, as we will see, tours of the Highlands did not begin to include the Trossachs until the closing years of the eighteenth century. When Coleridge and the Wordsworths asked directions to Loch Katrine at Tarbet in 1803, 'nobody seemed to know anything distinctly of the place, though it was but ten miles off', and when they arrived on foot, tired and hungry, at the remote western head of Loch Katrine on the evening of Friday 26

August the residents of a lonely house there were amused and bemused at the appearance of English travellers:

> A laugh was on every face when William said we were come to see the Trossachs; no doubt they thought we had better have stayed at our own homes. William endeavoured to make it appear not so very foolish, by informing them that it was a place much celebrated in England, though perhaps little thought of by them, and that we only differed from many of our countrymen in having come the wrong way in consequence of an erroneous direction.[7]

This exchange perhaps indicates the mismatch between the growing Romantic myth of the Scottish Highlands and the lived reality.[8] And Wordsworth was clearly overstating the Trossachs' celebrity in order not to look foolish. Nevertheless, we will see that there was some basis for claiming that the locality had recently achieved minor celebrity status in England.

An examination of the major published tours of and guidebooks to the Highlands of Scotland in the eighteenth century indicates that the Trossachs and Loch Katrine were almost wholly overlooked by Highland travellers until the late 1790s. Neither Daniel Defoe's *A Tour Through the Whole Island of Great Britain* (1724–26) nor Samuel Johnson's *Journey to the Western Isles of Scotland* (1775) makes any mention of the Trossachs or Loch Katrine. Thomas Pennant's *A Tour in Scotland, 1769* (1771) celebrates the beauties of Loch Awe, Loch Fine, Loch Long, and Loch Lomond but makes no mention of Loch Katrine.[9] In his later *A Tour in Scotland and Voyage to the Hebrides, 1772* (1774, 1776), Pennant climbs Ben Lomond and glimpses 'Loch Ketting' from the summit, but shows no interest in visiting the loch.[10] William Gilpin's two-volume *Observations, Relative Chiefly to Picturesque Beauty, Made in the Year 1776, On Several Parts of Great Britain; Particularly the High-Lands of Scotland* (1789) claims that Loch Lomond 'has ever been esteemed one of the most celebrated scenes in Scotland' (II, p. 15), but does not mention the scenes of Loch Katrine or the Trossachs. The same omission can be found in Tobias Smollett's *The Expedition of Humphry Clinker* (1771), the most important novelistic representation of Highland Scotland prior to Scott's Waverley Novels. Smollett's celebration of Loch Lomond is unsurprising, given that he grew up in the area, but this makes his neglect of Loch Katrine and the Trossachs all the more striking.

The same story can be found in the guidebooks to the Highlands that began to appear from the 1770s onwards, even those produced or written locally. In its entry for 'Dumbartonshire', Charles Burlington's pioneering guidebook *The Modern Universal British Traveller* (1779) announces that this shire 'exhibits many delightful and romantic scenes, among which is Lochlomond, one of the most beautiful pieces of water in the universe', but neither Loch Katrine nor the Trossachs are deemed worthy of observation in this or any other section of the book.[11] Twelve years later, the first edition of Robert Heron's *Scotland Delineated, or a Geographical Description of every Shire in Scotland* (1791) delineates Loch Lomond and Ben Lomond but not Loch Katrine or the Trossachs.[12] Likewise, Charles Ross's *The Traveller's Guide to Lochlomond, and its Environs* (1792) devotes over a hundred pages to Loch Lomond and Ben Lomond, but does not consider Loch Katrine and the Trossachs as noteworthy features of their environs.[13] The available evidence, then, indicates that while Loch Lomond was a well-established and celebrated part of the eighteenth-century Highland tour, Loch Katrine and the Trossachs were virtually unknown even in the early 1790s. If Loch Katrine and the Trossachs were places much-celebrated in England in 1803, ten years earlier they were not even on the tourist map.

Yet a few travellers did begin to find their way to the Trossachs in the second half of the 1790s, and some of them wrote tours and guidebooks that paved the way for Coleridge and the Wordsworths in 1803 and Scott in 1809. In this chapter I want to examine some of these tours and guidebooks in order to reiterate and develop my recent argument that the pioneering cultural work that began the process of fashioning the Trossachs and Loch Katrine into one of the key Romantic localities in Scotland was carried out by Robertson's report on the 'Parish of Callander', written in 1791 and published in 1794 in the *Statistical Account of Scotland*.[14] Although some nineteenth-century writers recognised Robertson as the 'discoverer' of the Trossachs, recent academic work on Trossachs tourism prior to *The Lady of the Lake* tends to ignore, deny or play down Robertson's impact.[15] In this chapter I reassert the nineteenth-century view by showing that, if Robertson was not literally the first discoverer of Loch Katrine and the Trossachs, then he was the first to celebrate the landscape of the area in print, the first to establish the standard tourist route from Callander to Loch Katrine, and – I will go on to suggest – the writer of the first guidebook dedicated to the region.

The Reverend James Robertson's Report on the 'Parish of Callander'

Robertson opens his account of the 'Romantic Prospects' of his parish by announcing that 'The Trosacks are often visited by persons of taste, who are desirous of seeing nature in her rudest and most unpolished state', and he closes it by informing his readers that the owners and residents of Loch Katrine's environs were already providing basic services for tourists: 'The Hon. Mrs DRUMMOND of PERTH has erected booths of wicker work, in the most convenient places, for the accommodation of strangers, who visit this wild and picturesque landscape; and the tenants of the next farm are very ready to show the beauties of the place to travellers' (Robertson, *Statistical Account*, vol. XII, pp. 139, 141–2). But while persons of taste may already have been visiting the Trossachs when Robertson wrote this in 1791, none of them appear to have published an account of their experiences. Shortly after his parish report appeared in 1794, however, these places had become a crucial part of almost every published tour and began to figure prominently in guidebooks. As we will see, the direct or indirect impact of Robertson's parish report is apparent in most of these tours and guidebooks, though it often went unacknowledged. We will also see that Robertson's parish report appears to have encouraged and shaped travellers' visits to this new Romantic hot spot through the way it was rewritten to form the first guidebook to the region.

Robertson's parish report may be said to invent the Trossachs' tourist and the standard itinerary by adopting the point of view of an imaginary traveller journeying westwards from Callander along what is now the A821 towards the Trossachs and Loch Katrine, passing Ben Ledi, Loch Venachar, Glen Finglas and Loch Achray on the way (pp. 139–40). As Robertson brings his traveller and his reader into the Trossachs, he raises the pitch of the aesthetic response:

> When you enter the *Trosachs*, there is such an assemblage of wildness and of rude grandeur, as beggars all description, and fills the mind with the most sublime conceptions. It seems as if a whole mountain had been torn in pieces, and frittererd down by a convulsion of the earth; and the huge fragments of rocks, and woods, and hills, scattered in confusion, for two miles, into the E. end, and on the sides of *Loch-Catherine*. The access to the lake is through a narrow pass, of half a mile in length, such as *Æneas* had in his dreary passage

to visit his father's home, '*vastoque immanis hiatu*'. The rocks are of
a stupendous height, and seem ready to close above the traveller's
head, or to fall down and bury him in their ruins. A huge column of
these rocks was, some years ago, torn with thunder, and lies in large
blocks very near the road [...]. The sensible horizon is bounded by
[...] weeping birches, on the summit of every hill, through which
you see the motion of the clouds, as they shoot across behind them.
(pp. 140–1)

Robertson's use of the aesthetic discourse of the Romantic tourist is
heightened through the trope of indescribability – invoked here through
an allusion to the claim in *Antony and Cleopatra* that Cleopatra's 'person/
[...] beggared all description' (II, 2, 202–3). This device suggests that the
physical features of the Trossachs' landscape are too sublime to be contained
by the descriptions and sketches of the picturesque tourist. Although indescribability had become a conventional indicator of the sublime since
Edmund Burke's *A Philosophical Enquiry into the Origin of our Ideas of the
Sublime and Beautiful* (1757/59), it is notable that the only significant use
of Shakespeare's phrase to refer to sublime landscape prior to Robertson's
use here was in Arthur Young's *A Six Months Tour Through the North of
England* (1770).[16] It is thus revealing that most subsequent writers about the
Trossachs prior to Scott echo Robertson's trope, sometimes employing his
allusion and sometimes acknowledging that they are doing so. Robertson
also sets a trend by endowing Loch Katrine with a supernatural aura, in this
case derived from classical literature, to match the supernatural wonders of
Loch Lomond. The quotation from Virgil's *Aeneid* (VI, 237) likens the pass
through to Loch Katrine to the 'vast, gaping opening' into the underworld
through which Aeneas passes to meet the shade of his father, making Loch
Katrine into a kind of Elysium. This suggestion is developed by a guidebook
voice: 'Travellers, who wish to see all they can of this singular phenomenon
[Loch Katrine], generally sail W. on the S. side of the lake, to the *Rock and
Den of the Ghost*, whose dark recesses, from their gloomy appearance, the
imagination of superstition conceived to be the habitation of supernatural
beings' (p. 141). Robertson goes on to describe, in minute detail, antici-
pating later descriptions of Romantic tourists, the aesthetic experience of
sailing along the loch or walking westwards along the track that runs along
the loch's northern shore (the Wordsworths' evening hike along this track

towards the shelter of a ferryman's cottage provided the stimulus for the poem 'Stepping Westward').

Robertson's Impact on Guidebooks

There is evidence to show that, although Robertson's parish report appeared as part of the expensive multi-volume *Statistical Account of Scotland* and was not likely to be carried on a tour, it nonetheless had a direct impact on some of the guidebooks written shortly afterwards by Scottish authors. In James M'Nair's *A Guide from Glasgow to Some of the Most Remarkable Scenes in the Highlands of Scotland* (1797) the entry on Callander includes a long footnote about Ben Ledi consisting of a substantial quotation from Robertson's parish report, and the descriptions of the Trossachs and Loch Katrine are clearly influenced by Robertson, including the sugges- tion that the scene is 'indescribably sublime'.[17] *The Traveller's Guide; or, a Topographical Description of Scotland* (1798) includes a description of the Callander area that is explicitly influenced by Robertson's report: after noting that 'The wild and romantic scenery and the noble prospects here are much admired' and that 'The Trossachs and the banks of Loch Ketterin almost exceed description', *The Traveller's Guide* adds a footnote consisting of a substantial quotation from Robertson.[18] Similarly, Thomas Garnett's account of the 'Village of Callander' in his two-volume *Observations on a Tour through the Highlands and Part of the Western Isles of Scotland* (1800) includes three quotations from Robertson in footnotes (pp. 170, 172, 173), and in recounting his visit to the Trossachs and Loch Katrine he tells us that 'it is impossible by words to convey any idea of the kind of scenery' (p. 174). Robertson's impact can also be seen in the second edition of Robert Heron's *Scotland Delineated* (1799); as we saw earlier, Loch Katrine and the Trossachs were not included in the first edition of 1791, but Heron inserted the following passage in the second edition: 'The beautiful and picturesque scenery known by the name of the *Trosachs*, at the east end of Loch Ketterin, merits notice. [...] Every object that can affect the mind with ideas of the rude grandeur and sublimity of Nature seems here assembled; and no traveller of taste can view this scene without delight and astonishment.'[19] That Heron had only recently become aware of Loch Katrine and the Trossachs is revealed by the absence of any mention of them in his *Scotland Described: or, a Topographical Description of all the Counties of Scotland* published two years earlier in 1797.[20]

Sarah Murray

The first important tour written by an English traveller who visited Loch Katrine and the Trossachs was Sarah Murray's *A Companion, and Useful Guide to the Beauties of Scotland* (1799), which records the 2000 mile solitary tour of Scotland that Murray undertook in the summer of 1796.[21] Although Loch Katrine and the Trossachs had begun to appear in guidebooks from 1797 onwards, Watson reports that Murray's account of her 1796 tour is the first she has found 'that extends the genre of the tour to the area' (*The Literary Tourist*, p. 226, n. 52). Murray went out of her way to visit 'the surrounding scenes of Loch Catheine', which she had been informed 'were more romantic than any other in Scotland' (*Companion, and Useful Guide*, p. 147). She does not tell us who gave her this information, but the close correspondences between her account of Callander and its environs with that of Robertson's parish report indicates that she had read that report or gained access to its information and even its language in some other way.

A Companion, and Useful Guide is as much about Murray herself – her intrepid feats and capacity for sublime response and action – as it is about the places she visits, and she is very much concerned to represent herself as a discoverer and pioneer. This is especially the case with the Trossachs and Loch Katrine where, like a colonial explorer, she named a vantage point after herself. John Leyden's journal entry for 16 July 1800 records an encounter with 'Mrs Murray of Kensington', then on a second Highland tour, at Loch Katrine: 'She conducted us to Murray Point, named from herself, the discoverer; whence we had an enchanting view of part of the Trosachs and of the greater part of the lake'.[22] In his edition of Wordsworth's *Recollections of a Tour Made in Scotland*, Shairp indicates that Murray also disputed with Robertson the honour of being the discoverer of the loch and its surroundings:

> [Elizabeth Isabella] Spence in her 'Caledonian Excursions,' 1811, says that the Honourable Mrs Murray told the minister of Callander that Scott ought to have dedicated 'The Lady of the Lake' to her as the discoverer of the Trossachs – 'Pray, Madam,' said the good doctor, 'when did you write your Tour?' 'In the year 1794.' 'Then, Madam, it is no presumption in me to consider that I was the person who in 1790 made the Trossachs first known, for except to the natives and a few individuals in this neighbourhood, this remarkable place had never been heard of.' (p. 314, n. 10)

In his *The Trossachs in Literature and Tradition* William Wilson highlights 'the free and easy inaccuracy of years' in this reported exchange and suggests that if Robertson had read Murray's book and noted how much it borrows from his own account of the region then 'his avoidance of the obvious retort, is a very pretty bit of courtesy.'[23] The inaccuracy of dates may, of course, have been introduced by Spence, but given Murray's concern for precedence it is possible that she may have antedated the year in which she wrote her tour (to two years before she undertook it) in order to make good her claim to be the discoverer of the Trossachs. Robertson's reply trumps her, even though it too claims an earlier date of composition than was strictly accurate. The anecdote is also intriguing in that it indicates that Murray met Robertson at some point between the publication of *The Lady of the Lake* in 1810 and her death in 1811. Whether or not they also met when Murray toured Scotland in 1796 and 1800 is a matter of conjecture. As we will see, however, there is evidence to suggest that Robertson was well aware of Murray and that he did indeed read her book soon after it was published.

Given her anxiety over priority, it is not surprising that Murray makes no mention of Robertson or his parish report in *A Companion and Useful Guide.* Yet the whole account of her daytrip to the Trossachs from Callander in chapter four is suffused with unacknowledged borrowings from Roberston. Murray follows Robertson's imaginary tourist from Callander to Loch Katrine, notices many of the same features (including the fact that the crags of Ben Ledi are made of 'plum-pudding stone'), repeats the indescribability trope, figures the pass through to the Loch as a passage to heaven or to hell, and exhibits even more sublime responses.[24] (The day after visiting the Trossachs, Murray visited Brackland Brig over the water of Kelty, which was another sublime feature in the locality pointed out by Robertson.[25])

Murray's account is fashioned to represent herself as an intrepid Romantic explorer. As she follows the route from Callander to Loch Katrine detailed by Robertson, Murray transforms the journey into a sublime quest through a landscape made all the more terrifying by heavy rain and torrents 'rushing' in chasms that threaten to swallow up her carriage (p. 147). As she approaches the pass through the Trossachs to Loch Katrine, Murray, echoing Robertson's derivation of the meaning of 'Loch-a-chravy', raises the pitch still higher and reaches for the indescribability trope:

> The awfulness, the solemnity, and the sublimity, of the scene at the ford, and by Loch-a-chravy's side, to the entrance to the foot of Loch Catheine, is beyond, far beyond description, either of pen or pencil! nothing but the eye can convey to the mind such scenery: well may it be called Loch-a-chravy, the lake of the field of devotion. When I quitted the narrow road under the rocks, by the side of Loch-a-chravy, it became amazingly jumbling, and winding, amongst various shaped rocks and crags, covered with wood; and rended chasms, deep and dark on every side; no trace of man, or living thing to be seen; every sound reverberated from rock to rock, flying through the gloomy labyrinth to announce the approach of unhallowed steps. My heart was raised in awe to heaven's solemnity; whilst that of my poor man was depressed to the dread of hell.[26] (p. 149)

Whereas Robertson characterises the supernatural aura of the pass through to Loch Katrine via classical allusion, likening it to a passage to the underworld, Murray figures it in Christian terms as a passage to heaven or hell. The contrast between her response and that of her 'poor man' allows Murray to figure herself as a heroic explorer capable of being exalted by terrifying landscapes that overwhelm or deflate those not conditioned by modern aesthetic taste to relish the delight of terror. Indeed, she goes on to say that she led her servants through the pass 'as the fittest person to encounter the devils, should they have taken possession of the field of devotion' (p. 150). Needless to say, she is 'astonished' and 'delighted' by the 'first glance of Loch Catheine' (p. 150), and while she waited to be rowed onto the loch by some men who happened to be unloading wood she climbs to a high point (later to be called 'Murray Point') in order to survey the beauty of the loch and the sublimity of the outlet 'through the awful pass to Loch-a-chravy' (p. 151). When the men take her onto the loch they row her, as Robertson advised, 'to the Den of the Ghost' (p. 152).

Robertson's Guidebook?

It seems, then, that Robertson's parish report on Callander had a direct impact on Murray's *Companion, and Useful Guide* and on several guidebooks to the Highlands published in the late 1790s. This in itself is quite remarkable, given that the *Statistical Account of Scotland* was expensive, had a limited print run and did not sell well.[27] Yet there was another way that

Robertson's parish report had an impact on early tours of Loch Katrine and the Trossachs since it appears to have formed the basis of the first published guidebook dedicated to the region – the anonymous *A Sketch of the Most Remarkable Scenery near Callander of Monteath*, first published in 1800 and problematically attributed to Margaret Oswald.[28] This pamphlet is so closely based on Robertson's parish report that it is either plagiarised from it or was written by Robertson himself – as some earlier writers have suggested.[29] I have noted about twenty echoes of or virtual quotations from Robertson's parish report in the twenty or so pages of this pamphlet. Perhaps the most obvious correlation is that the pamphlet's account of the pass through the Trossachs to Loch Katrine uses the same classical quotation as Robertson:

> At the entrance of that ravine, which leads to Loch Catherine, the sides are like immense walls, towering up to the clouds: the shivering rocks hang outward, ready to fall down: great blocks are strewed in the bottom of the defile, on both sides of the road. – Wood grows wherever there is any soil. – The clouds are seen shooting swiftly behind the trees, on the tops of hills: the echo is repeated to the stroke of the workman's ax, to the human voice, or to the rattling of the wheels of a carriage. This chasm, lofty, steep, craggy, and wild, *vastoque immanis hiatu*, which is about three furlongs in length, leads the traveller to the end of Loch Catherine. (p. 17)

As well as repeating the quotation from Virgil, this passage echoes several observations from Robertson's account of the pass in his parish report, including the blocks of stone strewing the bottom of the defile and the way the clouds can be seen shooting swiftly behind the trees on the ridges.

The most important impact of *A Sketch of the Most Remarkable Scenery near Callander* seems to have been upon Dorothy Wordsworth's *Recollections of a Tour Made in Scotland*. In fact, Wordsworth presents further evidence in support of the supposition that Robertson was the author of this pamphlet guidebook. As they prepare to approach the Trossachs and Loch Katrine for the second time, this time from the 'proper' direction established by Robertson, Wordsworth tells us that a waiter in Callander 'presented us with a pamphlet descriptive of the neighbourhood of Callander, which we brought away with us, and I am very sorry I lost it' (*Recollections*, p. 179). Wordsworth seems to have read the pamphlet before she lost it because she makes use of its description of the Trossachs in her retrospective account of Coleridge and the Wordsworths' first encounter with the Trossachs mentioned earlier. At the climax of her description, Wordsworth recalls 'a sentence in a little pamphlet written by the minister of Callander, descriptive of the environs of that place. After having taken up at least six closely printed pages with the Trossachs, he concludes thus, "In a word, the Trossachs beggar all description," – a conclusion in which everybody who has been there will agree with him' (*Recollections*, p. 104).[30] As we have seen, Robertson does say in his parish report that the assemblage of wildness and rude grandeur of the Trossachs 'beggars all description', but a report in a volume of *The Statistical Account of Scotland* can hardly be called 'a little pamphlet'. But *A Sketch of the Most Remarkable Scenery near Callander* fits Wordsworth's description pretty well. After about seven closely printed pages on the Trossachs, the writer does indeed conclude that 'The Trosachs beggar all description'.[31] Wordsworth is not then, as Louis Stott suggests, misquoting Robertson's parish report but accurately quoting the later guidebook that he based on his parish report.[32]

A Sketch of the Most Remarkable Scenery near Callander is of great interest in its own right, apart from the impact it had on the most famous literary visitors to Loch Katrine prior to Scott. Given Murray's attempt to claim priority over the discovery of the Trossachs and Loch Katrine, it is fascinating that the pamphlet quotes (or slightly misquotes) Murray's account of crossing the Bridge of Brackland over the Kelty (see *Sketch*, pp. 10–11 and *Companion*, pp. 155–6) – a sublime feature that Robertson had drawn attention to in his parish report. If Robertson was the author of this pamphlet guide, then he must have read Murray's book immediately after it was published in order to quote from it in a pamphlet published one year later. There is also a perhaps delicious irony in the way the pamphlet directs the reader 'to the hill of the Honourable Mrs *Murray* of *Kensington*' in order to get the best view of Loch Katrine (p. 22). The pamphlet appears to have sold well to an increasing number of visitors. It went through six editions (up to 1815), with the fifth edition of 1811 being substantially revised to incorporate numerous quotations from *The Lady of the Lake*. Robertson, who died in 1812, thus lived to record the impact of Scott's poem on the region that he had put on the tourist map more than fifteen years earlier. (It is not clear who was responsible for the sixth edition of 1815.)

John Stoddart: Loch Katrine's Celebrity

The main influence on the Wordsworths and Coleridge's tour of Scotland in 1803 was not *A Sketch of the Most Remarkable Scenery near Callander* but John Stoddart's two-volume *Remarks on Local Scenery and Manners in Scotland During the years 1799 and 1800* (Edinburgh and London, 1801).[33] Stoddart completed a version of the Long Tour, but in the reverse direction to that of Pennant, Johnson and Gilpin, beginning with Loch Lomond and an ascent of Ben Lomond and then making a clockwise loop of Scotland from Tarbet that ended in the Trossachs and Loch Katrine, thus making them the climax of his Highland tour. Arriving at Callander from the north, as the Wordsworths would on their second approach to Loch Katrine, Stoddart reports that the 'celebrity of [Loch Katrine] rendered me anxious to visit it, and I lost no time in making the excursion' (II, 307). Inevitably, Stoddart follows the route from Callander described by Robertson and yet his description of Loch Katrine and the Trossachs does not appear to be directly influenced by Robertson's parish report:

> At the head of Loch Achray begins that wild confusion of craggy masses, which is called the Trosachs, and which grow upon the imagination as you proceed. These form, as it were, the portico to the wild scenery of Loch Ketterine, and on the borders of the lake, they serve as promontories, to the singularly indented bays, which form the peculiar character of this landscape. Many of these spots would have been inaccessible to the traveller, had not the noble proprietors, at a considerable expense, formed paths along the sides of the precipices, which overhang the water. (II, p. 307)

Perhaps the most revealing comment that Stoddart makes about Loch Katrine is that he visited it because of its 'celebrity' – a statement that was presumably the basis of William Wordsworth's pronouncement in 1803 that the Trossachs was a place much-celebrated in England. It seems likely that the loch's as yet limited celebrity in England had been created by the publication of Murray's tour in 1799, though, as we have seen, Murray's own exploration of the locality seems to have been shaped by Robertson's parish report of 1794. Clearly, Loch Katrine and the Trossachs had attained a degree of celebrity, in Scotland as well as in England, ten years before *The Lady of the Lake* made it celebrated throughout the world.

Notes

1 For accounts of the impact of Scott's poem on the perception of Loch Katrine and the Trossachs, see Nicola J. Watson, *The Literary Tourist* (Basingstoke: Palgrave Macmillan, 2006), pp. 150–63, and 'Readers of Romantic Locality: Tourists, Loch Katrine and *The Lady of the Lake*', in Christoph Bode and Jacqueline Labbe (eds.), *Romantic Localities: Europe Writes Place* (London: Pickering and Chatto, 2010), pp. 67–79.

2 John Campbell Shairp (ed.), *Dorothy Wordsworth, Recollections of a Tour Made in Scotland, AD 1803* (New York, 1874), pp. 314–15, n. 12.

3 Watson, *The Literary Tourist*, pp. 154, 151.

4 Letter from Sir John Sinclair to Walter Scott, 6 November 1810, quoted in editor's footnote to letter from Walter Scott to Joanna Baillie, 31 December 1810, in H. J. C. Grierson (ed.), *The Letters of Sir Walter Scott, 1808–1811* (London: Constable, 1932), pp. 419–20.

5 Reverend James Robertson, 'Parish of Callander', in Sir John Sinclair (ed.), *The Statistical Account of Scotland, Drawn up from the Communications of the Ministers of the Different Parishes* in 21 vols. (Edinburgh: William Creech, 1791–1799), vol. XI, pp. 574–627. The 'Old Statistical Account' has been reorganised and republished as *The Statistical Account of Scotland*, ed. D. J. Withrington and I. R. Grant *et al.*, in 20 vols. (Wakefield: EP Publishing, 1973–1983); Robertson's 'Parish of Callander' appears in volume XII, edited by Bruce Lenman (pp. 137–90), which is the edition used in the present essay. The Old Statistical Account is also available as an online version produced by EDINA at the University of Edinburgh.

6 Alastair J. Durie, *Scotland for the Holidays: Tourism in Scotland c. 1780–1939* (East Linton: Tuckwell, 2003), pp. 34–35. See T. C. Smout, 'Tours in the Scottish Highlands from the Eighteenth to the Twentieth Century', *Northern Scotland*, 5.2 (1983), pp. 99–121, and Malcolm Andrews, *The Search for the Picturesque: Landscape, Aesthetics and Tourism in Britain, 1760–1800* (Aldershot: Scolar, 1989), pp. 200–01. Also see Thomas Garnett, *Observations on a Tour through the Highlands and Part of the Western Isles of Scotland* (London, 1800), vol. I, p. 109.

7 Dorothy Wordsworth, *Recollections of a Tour Made in Scotland, AD 1803*, ed. Carol Kyros Walker (New Haven and London: Yale University Press, 1997), pp. 91, 97.

8 See Kristin Ott, 'Sublime Landscapes and Ancient Traditions: Eighteenth-Century Literary Tourism in Scotland', in Bode and Labbe (eds.), *Romantic Localities*, pp. 39–50.

9 Thomas Pennant, *A Tour in Scotland, 1769* (1771), intr. Brian D. Osborne (Edinburgh: Birlinn, 2000), pp. 150–2.

10 Thomas Pennant, *A Tour in Scotland and Voyage to the Hebrides, 1772* (1774, 1776), in 2 vols, ed. Andrew Simmons (Edinburgh: Birlinn, 1998), pp. 147–8.

11 Charles Burlington, David Llewellyn Rees and Alexander Murray, *The Modern Universal British Traveller; or, a New, Complete, and Accurate Tour through England, Wales, Scotland, and the Neighbouring Islands. Comprising all that is Worthy of Observation in Great Britain* (London: J. Cooke, 1779), p. 765.

12 See Robert Heron's *Scotland Delineated, or a Geographical Description of every Shire in Scotland, Including the Northern and Western Isles. With some Account of the Curiosities, Antiquities, and Present State of the Country. For the use of Young Persons* (Edinburgh: James Neill, 1791).

13 See Charles Ross, *The Traveller's Guide to Lochlomond, and its Environs. Illustrated with a Map* (Paisley, 1792).

14 See Tom Furniss, '"Plumb-Pudding Stone" and the Romantic Sublime: The Landscape and Geology of the Trossachs in The Statistical Account of Scotland (1791–99)', in Bode and Labbe (eds.), *Romantic Localities*, pp. 51–65.

15 In its entry on 'Trossachs', the *Ordnance Gazetteer of Scotland*, ed. F. H. Groome (Edinburgh: T. C. Jack, 1882–1885), describes Robertson as 'the discoverer of the Trossachs' beauties'. In *The Literary Tourist*, however, Watson appears to dismiss such claims (p. 226, n. 52), suggesting that they were based on Robertson's *General View of the Agriculture in the Southern Districts of the County of Perth* (London, 1794) and *General View of the Agriculture in the County of Perth* (Perth, 1799), neither of which mentions the Trossachs (*The Literary Tourist*, p. 226, n. 52).

16 See Arthur Young, *A Six Months Tour Through the North of England*, 4 vols. (London, Salisbury, and Edinburgh: W. Strahan, 1770), vol. 3, pp. 184–5.

17 See James M'Nair, *A Guide from Glasgow to Some of the Most Remarkable Scenes in the Highlands of Scotland and to the Falls of Clyde* (Glasgow: Courier Office, 1797), pp. 41–53 (pp. 42–44, 47).

18 [Anon], *The Traveller's Guide; or, a Topographical Description of Scotland* (Edinburgh: J. Fairbairn, 1798), pp. 169–70.

19 Robert Heron, *Scotland Delineated, or a Geographical Description of every Shire in Scotland, Including The Northern And Western Isles. With Some Account Of The Curiosities, Antiquities, And Present State Of The Country* (Edinburgh: T. Brown, 1799), p. 158.

20 Robert Heron, *Scotland Described: or, a Topographical Description of all the Counties of Scotland* (Edinburgh: T. Brown, 1797), pp. 148–9.

21 See Sarah Murray, *A Companion, and Useful Guide to the Beauties of Scotland, to the Lakes of Westmoreland, Cumberland, and Lancashire; and to the Curiosities in the District of Craven, in the West Riding of Yorkshire. To which is added, a more particular Description of Scotland, especially that part of it, called the Highlands. By the Hon. Mrs Murray, of Kensington* (London: G. Nicol, 1799). For a useful analysis of Murray's text, see Betty Hagglund, *Tourists and Travellers: Women's Non-Fictional Writing About Scotland, 1770–1830* (Bristol: Channel View, 2010), pp. 54–76.

22 John Leyden, *Journal of a Tour in the Highlands and Western Islands of Scotland in 1800*, ed. James Sinton (Edinburgh and London: Blackwood, 1903), pp. 15–16. Also see Louis Stott, *Ring of Words: The Trossachs* (Milton of Aberfoyle: Creag Darach Publications, 1997), p. 27.

23 William Wilson, *The Trossachs in Literature and Tradition* (Stirling, 1908), pp. 53–4.

24 See Murray, *Companion, and Useful Guide*, pp. 149–52; for Robertson's attention in his parish report to the plum-pudding stone around Callander, see Tom Furniss, '"Plumb-Pudding Stone" and the Romantic Sublime', in Bode and Labbe (eds.), *Romantic Localities*, pp. 51–65.

25 See Robertson, *Statistical Account*, vol. XII, pp. 153–4, and Murray, *Companion, and Useful Guide*, pp. 154–7.

26 For Robertson's explanation of the meaning of Loch Achray's name, see *Statistical Account*, XII, p. 146.

27 See Tom Furniss, '"Plumb-Pudding Stone" and the Romantic Sublime', *Romantic Localities*, p. 54.

28 See [Anon], *A Sketch of the Most Remarkable Scenery near Callander of Monteath; Particularly the Trossachs* (Stirling: C. Randall, 1800). The British Library's problematic attribution of this pamphlet to Margaret Oswald seems to arise from Samuel Halkett and John Laing, *Dictionary of Anonymous and Pseudonymous English Literature*, new and enlarged edition edited by James Kennedy, W.A. Smith and A.F. Johnson, volume 5 (London and Edinburgh: Oliver and Boyd, 1929), p. 284.

29 In its entries on 'Trossachs' and 'Katrine, Loch', the *Ordnance Gazetteer of Scotland* identifies Robertson as the author of *A Sketch of the Most Remarkable Scenery near Callander of*

Monteath. Also see note 10 in Shairp's edition of Wordsworth's *Recollections of a Tour Made in Scotland,* pp. 313–4.

30 In his edition of Wordsworth's *Recollections,* Shairp says that the fact that Robertson uses 'the very sentence quoted by Miss Wordsworth' leaves him in 'no doubt he was the author of the little pamphlet' (pp. 313–4, n. 10). Wilson echoes this claim, but confuses the pamphlet and the parish report (*Trossachs in Literature and Tradition,* p. 53). Watson wrongly attributes the pamphlet guide to Patrick Graham, the minister of Aberfoyle: 'By 1802, there were already enough […] travellers to galvanise the local minister of Aberfoyle into producing his own little guidebook to the area at the urging of "some travelling gentlemen", *Sketches descriptive of Picturesque Scenery, on the southern confines of Perthshire, including the Trosachs, Lochard & c.* […] It was Graham's little book that Dorothy Wordsworth was carrying on her tour of the Highlands in the company of her brother and their friend Coleridge in the summer of 1803' (*The Literary Tourist,* pp. 153–54). Yet Graham's *Sketches Descriptive of Picturesque Scenery, on the southern confines of Perthshire* (Edinburgh, 1806) was published in 1806 not 1802, and Wordsworth makes it clear that the pamphlet she quotes from was written by the minister of Callander, not Aberfoyle. Louis Stott claims that Graham 'published the first guide to the District which he prepared for the visit of Joseph Farington (1747–1821), artist and diarist, in 1792' (*Ring of Words: The Trossachs,* p. 5). This is a misleading suggestion since Graham never published the account of the district that he prepared for Farington. Instead, as the 'Advertisement' indicates, Graham used that unpublished account as the basis for *Sketches Descriptive of Picturesque Scenery* in 1806 (pp. x–xi). I am grateful to Louis Stott for alerting me to Patrick Graham's 'For I. Farington Esq. R.A.: Sketches of the Situation of the Country, and manners of the People, from the Source of the Forth, to Gartmore' (Fort William, The West Highland Museum, MS-E-24). These sketches were written in 1792, but even if they had been published at the time they would not have challenged Robertson's pioneer status since they include only two cursory references to Loch Katrine and do not mention the Trossachs.

31 [anon] *Sketch of the Most Remarkable Scenery near Callander,* p. 24.

32 See Stott, *Ring of Words: The Trossachs,* p. 27.

33 On the Wordsworths' acquaintance with Stoddart and his *Remarks,* see Duncan Wu, *Wordsworth's Reading, 1800–1815* (Cambridge and New York: Cambridge University Press, 1995), pp. 205–6.

Scott and tourism

ALASTAIR J. DURIE

Introduction

Between 1780 and 1830 tourism was transformed as an industry. There was a revolutionary change in scale: what had been an experience only for the elite few became an activity for every section of society by the later nineteenth century. There was a widening of direction; what had once been mainly focused on Europe became a much more diffuse stream. This was change powered by choice; more time and more free income and better transport meant more and more people could travel as they wished or were persuaded. And no destination in Europe benefited more than Scotland, a development in which Scott clearly played a very significant part. Scott's writings drew people to Scotland, and shaped where within Scotland they chose to visit. Reading Scott drew people to Scott-land: 'his books', says one recent assessment 'contributed significantly to the remarkable increase in Scottish tourism.'[1] His writing helped tourism elsewhere, at Kenilworth, for example, but Scotland was the prime beneficiary of Scott.

'Scott wrote the script for the promotion of Scottish tourism', conclude the Golds.[2] The effect of his novels and poetry was in the first place general, to sell Scotland as a romantic place to discover, sufficiently different to be intriguing, distant but not dangerous, a mix of the new and the already familiar. Scotland became 'Scott-land', and Scott's land Scotland. This was a homophonic connection made early. Stuart Kelly quotes from David Gray's Letters, 'published in 1836': 'I call that his "land" in which his bones are laid, but, sooth to say, the whole of Scotland is Scott-land'.[3] Katherine Haldane argues that Scott fashioned Scotland as the definitive romantic country becoming Scotland's foremost tourist guide. 'Visitors who were well acquainted with Scott's works could claim to be travelling in a place where they were already at home'.[4] Academics disagree as to whether the role of Scott has been beneficial in terms of Scottish culture and identity, but it is not in dispute that an effect of his writing was to reshape Scotland's image to the benefit of tourism to Scotland and within Scotland.

As with all marketing, there was – unconsciously – in Scott a degree of gloss: 'Scott-land is a Baedeker to an imaginary land.'[5] But in all destination marketing, the dream is always worth more than the reality, the means less important than the end. If the visitors come, then massaging is justified, and truth a secondary consideration. This was never more so than at this time, when a first generation of people were being encouraged to travel for pleasure, even if not all Scott's contemporaries shared that encouraging view: there is the anecdote to be found in James Hogg's *Malise's Journey to the Trossacks* of a crusty Highlander who grumbled that 'a Mr Scott had put all the people mad by printing a lying poem about man that never existed – What the d— was to be seen about the Trossacks more than a hundred other places – A few rocks and bushes, nothing else.'[6] Perhaps, but Scott made those rocks, rather than some others, a place to visit. And it could not be gainsaid that his writing had made a very substantial difference.

Scott's Scotland

Scott had a general effect, but while Scotland as a whole basked in the glow of his writing, some areas and localities clearly benefited more than others. It might be a specific place – Melrose Abbey or Jennie Dean's cottage, a locality such as the Trossachs or a broader area like the Borders. Nowhere, however, benefited more from Scott than the North: Scott's Highlands would become, according to Nicola J. Watson, 'a must see destination for the landscape tourist'.[7] It was Scott that helped, or so Robert Clyde considers, to create the Highland tourist industry.[8] Contemporaries recognised what value there was to Scott's writing. Places Scott wrote about, or used as settings for his poetry or prose, attracted visitors, from whom money could be made. Guides, innkeepers and coachmen were, therefore, all fans of Scott. And places that Scott had not written about wondered whether he could be persuaded to feature their locality. That writing could sell a place to visitors was a lesson that others drew: Washington Irvine heard in August 1817 from Scott of an aged woman at whose inn 'with but little custom' he was pausing for refreshment. Her attention to him was first rate, but what lay behind it was that she had heard that he was the gentleman who had written 'a bonnie book about Loch Katrine'. Could he not write a little about their lake also, she begged, as it had done the inn at Loch Katrine a 'muckle deal of good'?[9]

Whether it was Scott alone that drew a visitor, there is no doubt that a knowledge of Scott coloured for many their time in Scotland, and was an essential part of their experience. This was especially so for Americans and Europeans for whom enthusiasm for Scott was stronger and lasted longer than it did for the locals, as has been argued by Allison Lockwood[10] and others. This degree of connection is seen time and time again, with an example being that of an unknown English diarist who came to Scotland in successive summers. During his first short eight-day Scottish tour in August 1817,[11] the recently published *Rob Roy* was clearly very much in his mind when he visited Glasgow. The Cathedral he describes as 'a place rendered immortal by being designated the Laigh Kirk in the novel of Rob Roy'. The following year, as part of a 'Peep at the Highlands', he made a point of visiting Rob Roy's celebrated cave, 'where it is said that Walter Scott composed part of his tale called Rob Roy'.

There is no more powerful illustration and corroboration of the immediate impact of Scott's writing on tourism than the way that the publication of *The Lady of the Lake* in May 1810 led to a remarkable surge in tourists over the following months and years to Callander and the Trossachs. A Stirling physician, Dr Lucas, noted in his diary on 28 August 1810, that many strangers were 'passing through the town in their way to the Trossachs, a very wild romantic part of the country'.[12] And what was producing this 'mania', as he dubbed it, was Scott's poem. Within weeks of its appearance, travellers were making their way north: Mrs Grant of Laggan had warning early in June that two English ladies of her acquaintance were set on a trip to Loch Catherine (Katrine), and mid-September found her accompanying them from Stirling to the Trossachs, 'where all the world are going to disturb the wood-nymphs and emulate Walter Scott'. There is even some statistical evidence, drawn perhaps from an inspection of the visitors' register at the inn. Five hundred chaises had been here this summer, she reported from the inn at Callander.[13] Sir John Sinclair was of like mind as to the increase of tourists and its cause. In November he wrote to Scott after a visit to Loch Katrine to acknowledge that 'you have increased the number of visitors beyond measure'. He went on – not for nothing was he known as *Statistical* Sir John – to state that his was the 297th coach in the course of the year 'when there had never previously before been above 100'.[14]

Sir John's objective in writing to Scott was to persuade him to set a sequel to *The Lady of the Lake* – to be called *The Lady of the Sea* – in Sinclair's native Caithness in the hope of attracting like numbers of tourists to that remote locality. While Loch Katrine and the Trossachs stand out as prime beneficiaries of Scott, there were other places in Scotland which also benefited, though none, perhaps to the same extent. Some of these visitors by chaise or coach will not have travelled on their own, but in families and parties, and so the influx was substantial, particularly when concentrated in the summer months. While some were from England, others were Scots, discovering their own country. Scott did not just work his spell on English and foreign visitors, but on Scots who for the first time were turning their sights on their own country, rather than going south or to the Continent.

Tourism before Scott
It is sometimes asserted that Scott created tourism in Scotland. But Scotland as a tourist destination was already established before Scott. From the 1760s onwards, increasing numbers of visitors had made a northern tour rather than an expedition to the Continent. The British were beginning to explore the remoter parts of Britain,[15] a process periodically accelerated by war in Europe, which prevented travel there. The Grand Tour in Europe remained the first choice of higher levels of society. But what helped domestic tourism was a growing enthusiasm amongst professional and commercial society for the mini-tour, an excursion of weeks rather than months, which might be spent in France, or in the Lakes, or the North of Britain. An English lady noted in her journal of a tour from London in the summer of 1788 through Glasgow and the Central and Northern Scotland that people were coming north at a great rate: 'all the world, it seems is travelling to Scotland or Ireland.'[16] Highland Scotland – central and western rather than the far north – was a particular beneficiary, assisted by the growing value of the Highlander in military circles and a changed perspective on the Jacobite cause, which had moved from being a handicap to an asset. The innkeeper at Fort William, where the young French aristocrat Rochefoucauld and his Polish tutor stayed in 1786, had been with Prince Charles's army at Culloden.[17] Or so he claimed, as did many others. The losing side had become the gallant cause. Another major ingredient was Ossian: Malcolm Andrews observes that the 'Ossianic cult drew tourists into the Highland regions'.[18] By the 1790s there was a growing number of tourists, hundreds rather than tens of thousands,

male and female, young and old, mostly British but a few Continental, to be found every summer in the north. At the turn of the eighteenth century, that redoubtable traveller Mrs Murray of Kensington happened across three German gentlemen on their way to Staffa,[19] drawn no doubt by the lure of Ossian. And this growth came despite the unpleasant reality that in many places the roads were no more than tracks, coaches uncomfortable, the inns dirty, and the ferrymen unreliable.

The fact was that by the later eighteenth century Scotland – before Scott – was becoming very fashionable. Edinburgh, the Athens of the North, was already a city of culture, but it was outside the Lowlands that the growth was most remarkable. It is astonishing how quickly – in under one generation – repression after the '45 Rising had given away to romanticisation of the Highlands. Highland scenery became picturesque; the Highlands a desirable playground for Southern sportsmen; Highland houses a summer residence (especially the more modern and less draughty) for the posh English visitor who came armed with a letter of introduction to their hosts with whom they expected to lodge free of charge. The Earl of Breadalbane noted ruefully in 1759 during the Seven Years War that his dinner table had been crowded with southern visitors: 'it has been the fashion this year to travel in to the Highlands.' Noblesse obliged him to be hospitable. Scottish landowners responded by laying out gardens and walks, building follies and hermitages, Ossianic halls, and showing the art treasures acquired on the Grand Tour. Most of their visitors were from the top drawer, but, even so, amongst the instructions to the guides at Dunkeld was that the picking of flowers by visitors was not to be permitted.

The flow north was shaped by the increasing numbers of guidebooks and accounts of Scotland that became available in print in England and in Europe by as early as the 1790s as Nenadic has shown.[20] Although the relationship between the number of published accounts, their readership and actual travel is not a straight correlation, some did convert their interest into travel. Scott himself recognised in July 1810 how the numbers of visitors had grown; 'an age when every London citizen makes Loch Lomond his washpot.'[21]

Scott and Tourism: some qualifications.

There is a danger, however, of overstating Scott's importance. First, not everyone who read Scott went on to visit Scotland. Armchair travellers, whether European or English, often remained just that; many could or would not convert from journeys of the mind to real time. The very successful English novelist Charlotte Yonge is an example. She had the time, the money and the health to travel, and an immense enthusiasm for Scott, whom she quoted more than any other author, including Shakespeare. Yet she never visited Scotland.[22] Second, Scott may not have been the determining factor in a visitor choosing Scotland, although his writing certainly persuaded people that Scotland could and perhaps should be visited. Mrs Mary Thompson is a case in point. Wife of a Hull banker, with her son, she made a two-month tour in Scotland during the summer of 1807, what she called her 'northern tour' took her to Edinburgh and then to Dunkeld and Inveraray before returning by way of Glasgow. She knew Scott's *Lay of the Last Minstrel* and that must have been why she went out of her way to visit Melrose where she was shown round the Abbey by an intelligent man who had the poem 'at his finger ends, and expressed his obligation to that writer for a great increase in visitants'.[23] But her diary opens with a quotation from Johnson, and her observations suggest an interest in the Scots, more than in Scott. Her interest was in the people and their customs, more than in prose or poetry.

It is tempting too, because such letters and journals have survived, to assume that all tourists were on a literary and cultural tour. That is what the word 'tourist' had meant in Europe (cf. Pope's 'The Grand Tourist'), a particular type of traveller: 'a traveller now is called a touri-ist'.[24] But the definition was widening to take in a much wider range of travel for pleasure and leisure, those who came for sport or science, for the seaside or the hills, for education and for health. In a diary entry at Oban written in September 1840, Lord Cockburn summed up the variety of tourists that he had encountered in his recent judicial travels.

> The number of foreign but chiefly of English travellers is extraor-
> dinary [...] attracted by scenery, curiosity, superfluous time and
> wealth, and the fascination of Scott while attracted by grouse, the
> mansion houses of half of our poor devils of Highland lairds are
> occupied by rich and titled Southrons. Even the students of Oxford
> and Cambridge come to the remote villages of Scotland to study.[25]

Cockburn's comment is important in helping us to assess what Scott did contribute to Scottish tourism, and equally to recognise what he did not.

'The fascination of Scott', in Cockburn's phrase, was one feature, but not the only factor in drawing people to Scotland. Not all tourism or visitors were driven by culture. Health was a driving force whether for invalids over-wintering in milder climes at Torquay or Nice, or looking for relief from complaints such as gout or arthritis. There was the long established practice of 'taking the waters', although for most who could afford the cure, this meant travelling away from Scotland to Bath or a Continental spa. It remained a reality that Scottish spas, of which there were a number, were essentially of very limited appeal and in consequence lacked both accommodation and amenities. Scott's mother and sister had to abort a projected visit in September 1794 to Innerleithen because there were no lodgings to be had.[26] Scots mostly went south or abroad for spa treatment, and no European would have looked to Moffat or Bridge of Earn rather than their own spas. It might be true that, as one authoritative health guide said, that the 'Springs known as St Ronan's Well are much celebrated by their general identification with the scene of one of Sir Walter Scott's novels', but that did not convert into significant numbers or commercial success.[27] His view of spas was not very positive, although he had personal experience of several, both major (Bath) and minor (Gilsland): 'moping about some watering place'[28] does not sound enthusiastic.

There was also the new vogue spread from England into Scotland for the salt water cure, drinking seawater and dipping, or being ducked. Bathing machines were making their appearance at some Scottish seaside resorts, and it would be surprising indeed if some had not been drawn up above the high water mark when Scott was riding on Portobello sands in the autumn of 1807.[29] He stayed in Gundimore, the marine villa of his friend, Mr William Rose, at Mudeford in Hampshire. The seaside was beginning to attract not just upper and middle class invalids, but day-trippers and pleasure-seekers of all classes. Yet Scott ignored the possibilities of a sea-bathing resort as a location for his writing: it was a new phenomenon, not part of the past with which he was concerned. Not for him a Sanditon. It may be that personal experience coloured his indifference: 'Folks who have been nearly drowned in bathing rarely venturing a second time out of their depth.'[30]

Sport was what put Scotland on the summer itinerary for an increasing number of visitors. Victorian Scotland, with its deer forests, grouse moors and salmon fishings, was to become Europe's sporting playground for the wealthy. Already, however, by the later eighteenth century there was a stream of sporting tourists from the south, with whom Scott was familiar. 'They came here occasionally as sportsmen to shoot moor game, without any idea of looking at scenery.'[31] Shooting and fishing drew these visitors, mostly young men,[32] and they seldom paid for their sport: commercialisation, the letting of moors, the renting of fishings and so on, was to set in from the 1820s, partially at least in response to rapidly rising numbers of itinerant sportsmen. While it was just a few, there were no great problems, as Scott's neighbour, the Cornish gentleman who had settled in Selkirkshire for the sake of the fishing, showed.[33] But the grouse shooting in the North was a growing attraction, with some Highland inns packed to overflowing on the eve of the Glorious Twelfth. Lord Cockburn thought in 1846 that the autumnal influx of sportsmen was a very recent occurrence, in his phrase they 'now coming in flocks', but the scouts were already arrived at the turn of the eighteenth century. The sporting tour of the Yorkshire squire, Colonel Thornton, which was published in 1804,[34] but was actually a composite of several sporting forays in the 1780s, did much to alert southern sportsmen to the potential of the north.

Scott understood the appeal of field sports for tourists, but his writing did not particularly promote this significant aspect of tourism. In no other country in Europe was sporting tourism to be such a major element until the advent of mountaineering and winter sports in Switzerland towards the end of the nineteenth century. On wet and Sabbath days sportsmen might read Scott, but it was sport, not writing, that had drawn them north. Dr Norman Macleod recalled a dinner party in London in May 1855 where he met with a party of parsons, most of them knowing nothing of Scotland 'except as a place in the Islands from which grouse come'.[35] That may well have been a more widely held view of what defined Scotland than that of the enthusiasts for Scott would allow. And the popularity of field sports was a critical element in the conversion of tourism to a commercial industry. Rising numbers and growing demand made the old conventions of freely offered hospitality no longer sustainable. Mrs Murray had wondered how the two hospitable gentlemen and their families at Aros on Mull, a jumping off point for many visitors to Staffa, would cope unless an inn was built. 'They must every year experience a heavier tax on their hospitality from an increase of travellers to the isles, with letters of introduction.'[36] Scott observed in 1810 that 'The number of English travellers have of late years made the Highland tours tolerable which they were not in my former visits to the mountains – so that we have no tales of hardships or even privation to tell you'.[37] Nonetheless, such change in provision and improvement had to be financed, and, whatever other motives for tourism there were, Scott's writing was what made the tipping point, when tourism in Scotland moved from custom to commerce, from hospitality to an industry.

Conclusion

It would be simply laziness, indeed, to agree that Scott invented Scottish tourism.[38] As we have seen, Scotland was already developing as a tourist destination before Scott. And while literary, cultural and scenic tourism was a significant dimension of this new industry, also expanding – and largely independent of Scott – were other important kinds of tourism, of which the sporting was the most notable. And there were other portals for the literary tourist – Ossian or Burns, perhaps. Nevertheless, if Scott was not the creator of tourism, his writing certainly acted as an accelerant. Contemporaries had no doubt as to Scott's importance to Scottish tourism. In the *Edinburgh Evening Courant*'s obituary of Scott,[39] full recognition was given to his role in the promotion of tourism.

> Thousands from foreign lands are yearly visiting our shores, to tread the localities which he has given to fame. Inns have been erected for the accommodation of travellers where, before his day, from the end of one year to the end of the next, the foot of a stranger never planted itself.

The case was made, and accepted in Scottish circles that indeed Scott was without rival in terms of the effects on tourism and travel that his literature produced.

> Cervantes has done much for Spain, and Shakespeare for England, but not a tithe of what Sir Walter Scott has accomplished for us. In each of these great writers we find many localities sanctified by their genius, in their respective countries; but that of Scott pervades every corner of his native land.

Tourism changed Scotland. Without Scott, there would still have been growth in tourism, but not as much nor as quickly. And what a godsend for marketing was the brand name: 'Scotland is Scott-land'. One wonders what might have been the effect had Walter Scott been called Walter Smith or Campbell.

Notes

1   Lynne Withey, *Grand Tours and Cook's Tours* (New York: Morrow, 1997), p. 55.
2   John and Margaret Gold, *Imagining Scotland, Tradition, Representation and Promotion in Scottish Tourism since 1750* (Aldershot: Scolar, 1995), p. 83.
3   Stuart Kelly, *Scott-land: The Man Who Invented A Nation* (Edinburgh: Polygon, 2010), p. 310. Kelly notes this phrase was also used by the American traveller Bayard Taylor, 'It was all Scott-land', in 1846, in *Views a-foot, or, Europe seen with knapsack and staff* (New York: G. P. Putnam, 1859), also cited by Allison Lockwood, *Passionate Pilgrims: The American Traveler in Great Britain, 1800–1914* (New York and London: Cornwall Books, 1981), p. 70. Kelly credits Alexander Smith in *A Summer in Skye* (London: Strahan, 1865 [dated by Kelly as 1856]) with originating the formulation, 'Scotland is Scott-land'.
4   Katherine Haldane Grenier, *Tourism and Identity in Scotland 1770–1914* (Aldershot: Scolar 2005), p. 80.
5   Stuart Kelly, *Scott-land: The Man Who Invented A Nation* (Edinburgh: Polygon, 2010), p. 2.
6   *The Spy*, 1 June 1811, cited in *Travel Writing 1700–1830: An Anthology* (Oxford: Oxford University Press, 2008).
7   Nicola J. Watson, *The Literary Tourist: Readers and Places in Romantic & Victorian Britain* (Basingstoke: Palgrave Macmillan, 2006), p. 50.
8   Robert Clyde, *From Rebel to Hero: the Image of the Highlander 1745–1830* (East Linton: Tuckwell, 1995) p. 122.
9   Washington Irving, *Abbotsford and Newstead Abbey* (London: John Murray, 1835), p. 186.
10 Lockwood, *Passionate Pilgrims*, especially pp. 65–78.
11 Glasgow City Archives, MS TD 637/1 *First Tour to the Highlands, 1817* and *[Second Tour] 1818*.
12 Stirling Archives, PD 16/4/2 *Diary of Dr Lucas*.
13 *Memoir and Correspondence of Mrs Grant of Laggan*, edited by her son, J. P. Grant, (London: Longman, Brown, Green and Longmans, 1844) vol. 1, pp. 267–9: Letter CVII, Stirling, 17 September 1810.
14 H. J. C. Grierson, *Letters of Sir Walter Scott: 1808–1811* (London: Constable, 1932), pp. 419–420: Scott to Joanna Baillie, 31 December 1810.
15 Malcolm Andrews, *The Search for the Picturesque: Landscape, Aesthetics and Tourism in Britain, 1760–1800* (Aldershot: Scolar, 1989), chapter 8, pp. 197–240: 'The Highlands Tour and the Ossianic Sublime'.
16 Glasgow University Library, Special Collections MS Gen. 738: Mrs Diggle, *Journal of a tour from London to the Highlands of Scotland*, 19 April to 7 August 1788, Letter 23rd, Gretna.
17 Norman Scarfe, *To The Highlands in 1786: The Inquisitive Journey of a Young French Aristocrat* (Woodbridge: Boydell Press, 2001), p. 178.
18 Andrews, *Search*, p. 198.
19 Sarah Murray, *A Companion and Useful Guide to the Beauties of Scotland* (Hawick: Byways, 1982), p. 93.

20 Stana Nenadic, 'Land, the landed and relationships with England: literature and perception 1760–1830', in S. Connolly, R. Houston and R. J. Morris (eds.), *Conflict, Identity and Economic Development* (Preston: Carnegie, 1995), pp. 150–1.

21 Grierson, *Letters of Sir Walter Scott*, p. 357: Scott to John Richardson, 3 July 1810.

22 Kathleen Tillotson, 'Charlotte Yonge as a Critic of literature', in Georgina Battiscombe and Marghanita Laski (eds.), *A Chaplet for Charlotte Yonge* (London: Cresset Press, 1965), pp. 56–70. Tillotson quotes Yonge's remark that 'My prime literary affection must ever be for Sir Walter' (p. 60).

23 Arthur R. B. Robinson, *Seeking the Scots: An English Woman's Journey in 1807* (Skelton: A. R. B. Robinson, 2006), p. 25.

24 Samuel Pegge, *Anecdotes of the English Language*, (1800) cited in the *Oxford English Dictionary*.

25 Lord Cockburn, *Circuit Journeys*, (Hawick: Byways, 1983), p. 51.

26 John Gibson Lockhart, *Memoirs of Sir Walter Scott* (London: Macmillan, 1900), vol. I, p. 196: Walter Scott to his aunt, Miss Christian Rutherford, 5 September 1794: 'a killing post came from this fountain of health [informing] us no lodgings were to be had there.'

27 *Guide to the Inland Watering Places of Great Britain and Ireland* (London: Upcott Gill, 1891), p. III.

28 Lockhart, *Memoirs*, Vol. I, p. 202, 23 August 1795.

29 Lockhart, *Memoirs*, Vol. I, p. 465.

30 Grierson, *Letters*, p. 287: Scott to Lady Abercorn, 21 January 1810.

31 N. T. Willis, *Abbotsford* (London, 1854), p. 78.

32 Alastair J. Durie, 'Unconscious Benefactors: Grouse-shooting in Scotland', *International Journal of the History of Sport* (December 1998), pp. 38–9.

33 Lockhart, *Memoirs*, p. 343: Scott to George Ellis, 27 August 1803.

34 See Michael Brander, *A Hunt Around the Highlands* (Gloucester: Standfast Press, 1973). Scott was very unimpressed by the amount of equipment and supplies that Thornton took for his safari. 'Some of us do know where to find a bit of game, [but] having in our retinue neither two boats nor a skiff to travel by seas, nor a gig, two baggage wagons nor God knows how many horses for the land service.' *The Edinburgh Review*, 5, 1805, p. 399.

35 Donald MacLeod, *Memoir of Norman MacLeod, D.D.* (London, 1877), p. 254.

36 Sarah Murray, *A Companion and Useful Guide*, p. 146.

37 Grierson, *Letters*, Scott to George Ellis, 29 July 1810, p. 67.

38 Kelly, *Scott-land*, p. 95.

39 As reported in the *Stirling Journal*, 28 September 1832.

Holiday romances; or, Loch Katrine and the literary tourist

NICOLA J. WATSON

'What the d— was to be seen about the Trossacks more than in an hundred other places? [...] A few rocks and bushes, nothing else'.[1] If nothing else, James Hogg's remark voiced by an elderly and imaginary Highlander begs the question: how did it come about that *The Lady of the Lake* made a trip to Loch Katrine into a favoured excursion for practically everybody who was anybody (and many others besides) for over a hundred years? In this chapter I shall be enquiring into the ways that the poem itself initiated this impulse, and exploring how tourist interest inspired by *The Lady of the Lake* depended on ways in which the poem was subjected to cultural adaptation. On the one hand, the poem was simplified by and for its readers, in the sense that within cultural memory there was a tendency to reduce it to the scenes set in the environs of Loch Katrine; and it was elaborated by and for readers through contemporary practices of visual depiction, performance-adaptation, and tourism itself, all of which worked to bind poem and place together within the nineteenth-century imagination. As a result, for a hundred years after the publication of Scott's best-seller, it was impossible to see Loch Katrine other than suffused by Scott's romance, something acknowledged, however sardonically, by Hogg, whose tongue-in-cheek advice to contemporary tourists en route for the Trossachs in the early 1820s was 'let him have the 11th, 12th, and 13th divisions of the first canto of *The Lady of the Lake* in his heart; a little Highland whisky in his head; and then he shall see the most wonderful scene that nature ever produced'.[2] Forty years later, when the phenomenon was well-established, Charles Roger simply wrote, silently quoting the poem, 'To this land of mountain and flood, for many years *The Lady of the Lake* served as the only guide, and [...] it is still the tourist's best companion'.[3]

Although Loch Katrine as we experience it today is very much the product of the tourism that Scott's writing inspired, the scenery of the Trossachs and the loch had been known to the local gentry as a beauty-spot since around the 1780s. The landscape was commonly described in contemporary writings in terms of a mix of the sublime (the rocky defile of the pass of the Trossachs itself and the framing heights of Ben A'an and Ben Venue) and the beautiful (the unusually deep lake and the luxuriant framing trees and ferns). The scenery at that end of the lake lent itself to being thought of in the technical terms of William Gilpin's concept of the picturesque – in terms of a repertoire of foregrounds, glimpses, prospects, side-wings, and side-screens, in short, as something to be sketched. Alexander Campbell, among others, so describes it in 1802 in his *A Journey from Edinburgh through parts of North Britain*, recommending a series of 'stations' to the would-be artist, and remarking especially on the virtues of a boat on the lake for this purpose. Dorothy Wordsworth would echo this sentiment in her account of her trip with her brother down the lake from west to east in 1803, noting that their boatman always chose the 'bonniest' part 'with greater skill than our prospect-hunters and "picturesque travellers"'.⁴ As her comment on the boatman's practised patter suggests, the locale was already organised as a destination for a select number of picturesque enthusiasts by 1799; the land-owners had blasted a lakeside road through the boulders that had hitherto obstructed access and could only previously be accessed by a complicated set of ladders; and they had installed two wicker picnic shelters to protect visitors from the rain.⁵ Mentioned by James Robertson in his *Statistical Account of Scotland* (1794), by 1799, the locality was already being written about in books conceived explicitly as guidebooks, such as *The Traveller's Guide: or, a Topographical Description of Scotland [...]* (1798), Sarah Murray's *A Companion, and Useful Guide to the Beauties of Scotland* (1799), *A Sketch of the Most Remarkable Scenery near Callender* (often attributed to Margaret Oswald, 1800, although possibly by Robertson), and *Sketches descriptive of Picturesque Scenery [...] including the Trosachs, Loch Ard etc.* (1806) by Patrick Graham, the local minister of Aberfoyle.⁶ Graham's remarks on how to enjoy the defile of the Trossachs suggest forcefully how, before 1810, the excursion was primarily conceived as a pictorial experience, available to the disciplined eye:

> On entering the Trosachs let him remark on the right, the beautiful disposition into which Nature has thrown the birches and the oaks which adorn the projecting cliffs; let him remark the grouping of the trees, with their elegant figure and form. Some aged weeping birches will attract his eye; Binnan, and Benivenow, will present, at every step, varied pictures. In passing through the dark ravine that opens

on Loch Ketturin, [...] he admires the disposition of the birches, the
hawthorns, the hasles, and oaks and mountain ashes ...[7]

In 1809, then, when Scott travelled through the area on holiday, he
was travelling not just to somewhere he had visited three times before (in
1790, 1793, and 1796), but along an already well-defined tourist route for
lovers of scenery. He began to write *The Lady of the Lake* while staying at
Cambusmore house in the locality. Published in May of 1810, it produced
an immediate tourist boom. In 1806 Patrick Graham estimated that there
were six or seven carriages a day arriving from Callander in the high season
for tourism between about May and November; by 1810, private letters and
diaries were putting the number at more like fifty a day, and in her *Sketches
of the Present Manners, Customs, and Scenery of Scotland* (1811) Elizabeth
Isabella Spence guessed that five hundred had come through by mid-August
of that year.[8] There was a corresponding increase in tourist amenities. By
1811, according to the fifth edition of *A Sketch of the Most Remarkable Scenery
Near Callender* (tellingly much expanded with quotation from *The Lady of
the Lake*) the wicker shelters had been supplemented by a new hotel at
Callander, a new inn at Lochearnhead, and an official guide (James Stuart)
who would row sight-seers out onto the lake in his boat. By the 1840s his
cottage had turned first into a 'public', and then into an inn; it was finally
rebuilt in 1855 as the Trossachs hotel, complete with turrets inspired by
Abbotsford. By 1858 there was a railway to Callander from which it was
possible to travel out by hired carriage, but it was also possible to take
day-trips by charabanc out of Edinburgh and Glasgow. By 1843 a small
steamer called *The Gypsy* was running on the loch (before then it had been
the oared launch *Water Witch*).

The evidence for a tourist boom is clear; less clear is why *The Lady of
the Lake* produced such instant tourist enthusiasm. One might postulate
some purely pragmatic explanations. On the one hand, the continuing
Napoleonic wars meant that travel in search of the pleasures of scenery was
confined to the British Isles. Moreover, Loch Katrine was, and is, relatively
convenient to the metropolitan centres on both the west and east sides of
Scotland – meaning that it can be accessed both by travellers coming up
from London and those (often international travellers) landing at Liverpool.
It was therefore a relatively accessible piece of the 'Highlands'.

There are, however, aesthetic explanations as well for the poem's ability to draw tourists, and these are to do with the content and form of the poem itself. To begin with, it is worth noting that *The Lady of the Lake* simply takes over the prevailing aesthetics of scenery-description. Canto 1's lengthy descriptions of the locale were hugely influential, and would be quoted at length in lieu of any other description in all subsequent nineteenth-century guidebooks. Indeed, overall Canto 1 was the part of the poem that seems to have been most influential in inspiring tourism. This is because it effectively provided models in its protagonists, its narrative, and its footnotes for the emergent tourist experience. Fitz-James, for example, models the tourist's arrival and adventure. His adventure models and traces the standard route of the eighteenth-century tourist into this landscape; he himself follows his pleasure as lightly, as whimsically as a tourist. Tourist-like, Fitz-James has an imperfect and irresponsible sense of the topography, physical, political, or emotional, of the place into which he has wandered. As it proves later in the poem, he is the king indulging himself in the pleasures of travelling incognito, pleasing himself with pretending to be a landless knight, a huntsman escaping to a land of Spenserian romance, indulging himself, therefore, in something very much like a tourist fantasy. His encounter with the Trossachs and its inhabitants involves a sentimental susceptibility to the charms of the lady of the lake and her island retreat.

If Fitz-James seems like a variant of the tourist, the incognito exiled Douglas household romantically living rough effectively model the ideal holiday escape from the everyday. Ellen presides over the perfect accommodation for the incognito king, embodying a sense that it is possible to escape everyday duties and responsibilities to somewhere secret, romantic, alternative, and temporary, a holiday house in which one's normal social identity can be cast aside, without forfeiting one's class privileges.[9] Although, as Ali Lumsden has remarked, the poem's narrative points out that this absorption into a space of romance, indeed of fairyland, is a dangerous fantasy indulged by the king (who will be thereby exposed to the deadly enmity of the rebel Roderick Dhu), and that political responsibility and identity weigh as heavily on the lady as on the huntsman, it simultaneously makes that fantasy of escape available and powerfully attractive to the reader.[10] The poem as a whole brings about an alliance between the Highlands and the king in Stirling castle, made possible by the king's unfulfilled *tendresse* for Ellen (whose virtuous marriage to Malcolm Graeme he finally enables, rather than himself pursuing her to make her his mistress). The poem thus models the tourist's relation to the landscape – attraction, flirtation, followed by a wistfully regretful romantic distance and discreet management of responsibility; as such, it is a real holiday romance.

If the poem models the tourist in its protagonists and its narrative, it also describes this romance within a framing discourse plundered and adapted from the genre of the guidebook. Scott embroiders the verse narrative with a mass of antiquarian footnotes drawn from contemporary guidebooks and topographical writings, including *A Sketch*, Campbell, Graham, and others. One result of this is that the narrative itself acquires at least a tinge of historical status – some of this story really did happen, and it really happened here. The footnotes encourage a practice of locating the fictional events described upon a real map; Scott remarks, for example, of the route of the sign for the clans to rise in support of the Douglas and Roderick Dhu, the Fiery Cross, that 'a glance at the provincial map of Perthshire, or at any large map of Scotland, will trace the progress of the signal [...]' (notes to Canto Third, p. lxiii).[11]

In these ways, the poem was well-placed to activate in its readers a desire not merely to read but to take the poem on holiday with them. It was perfectly in tune with other cultural trends. There had been, first of all, a recent history of tourist interest in sites associated with specifically fictive events. There had been a vogue for visiting locales around Lake Geneva associated with Rousseau's novel *La Nouvelle Helöise* (1761) which took off in the 1780s.[12] Scott's earlier narrative verse had already been producing some of this effect; in the wake of *The Lay of the Last Minstrel*, Melrose Abbey became ever more popular as a tourist destination. This literary tourist impulse can be related to something more nebulous and widespread, what Martin Meisel identifies as the twinned contemporary impulses towards 'realisation' and 'illustration' of texts characteristic of nineteenth-century culture.[13] The first, as described by Meisel, is a desire to 'materialise' the text in physical form; the second is a desire to extend and elaborate the text's own sense of itself, through providing additional material in the shape of further information both textual and visual. In practice, these two impulses defined and supported one another, as can be seen in the many adaptations of *The Lady of the Lake* for both public and private performance (in the forms of parlour music, private theatricals, civic cantatas, stage melodrama, and grand opera) and the extensive industry in 'illustrating' the poem, visualising its narrative and its setting and amplifying its antiquarian materials. Arguably, the practice of literary tourism to Loch Katrine was effectively simply a variant of the widespread contemporary practices of illustrating and adapting *The Lady of the Lake*; but equally it seems likely that it was fuelled by them.

In this respect it is of interest that both the illustration and the stage-adaptation of the poem show a marked tendency to improve on and underscore the poem's topographical specificity as the century wears on. The two different sets of illustrations first by Richard Westall and then by Richard Cook commissioned in 1810 and 1811 respectively were relatively uninterested in placing the poem within a recognisable topography. Westall's depiction of Ellen in her boat, for example, places her simply against a generic backdrop. Richard Cook's, a year later, is rather more place-specific, apparently showing Ben Venue rising in the background, but its main focus is the figures of Fitz-James and Ellen. But by 1822, topographical engravings of the locality made famous by Scott's poem, such as *Six Views of Loch Katrine* (1822) were being captioned with Scott's verses. By 1827, books mixing landscape and narrative illustration were beginning to appear. *Vues Pittoresques de l'Ecosse [...] par F. A. Pernot avec texte explicatif extrait en grande partie des ouvrages de Sir Walter Scott par A. Pichot* (1827) featured engravings depicting not only Loch Katrine as it appeared to the modern eye, but Loch Katrine represented with Fitz-James and his hunting dogs winding his horn in the foreground and Fitz-James and his dying 'gallant grey' against the backdrop of the Trossachs. This tendency to superimpose the narrative incidents and characters of the poem onto the verifiable topography of the place also characterises a publication of some ten years later. The engravings (possibly by Thomas Allom) are captioned as topographical depictions ('The Pass of the Trossachs' and 'Loch Katrine, looking towards Ellen's Isle') but what they show is, respectively, the dead horse and Fitz-James alone on the silver strand. A similar strategy informed Charles Tilt's publication of *Illustrations; Landscape, Historical, and Antiquarian to the Poetical Works of Sir Walter Scott, Bart.* (1834) which included a landscape of Ben Venue by G. F. Robson cheek-by-jowl with two depictions of the events of the poem, J. H. Nixon's 'Ellen Douglas and Fitz-James' in Ellen's bower and S. A. Hart's 'The Knight of Snowdoun'.[14] Robert Herdman's *Six Engravings in Illustration of the Lady of the Lake* (1868) included one showing

Ellen 'with Ellen's Isle, Loch Katrine, and part of the slopes of Ben Venue behind her.'[15] Throughout the rest of the century, visual depictions of Loch Katrine, whether fine art or cheap postcards, would generally reference *The Lady of the Lake*, if only by implication. The stag in James Trant Walton's 'Stag on Loch Katrine' (1850), for example, is clearly a descendant of Scott's stag. The ubiquitous empty boat drawn up on a beach regularly depicted in postcards of Loch Katrine silently references Ellen Douglas. Thus, when Scott and his publisher engaged J. M. W. Turner to illustrate the collected *Poetical Works* (1833) with topographical subjects, and Turner delivered a view of 'Loch Katrine' to act as a frontispiece to volume eight, Scott was effectively publishing his poems, including *The Lady of the Lake*, in a format designed to keep pace with and promote the development of the very tourist sensibility that they had instigated.[16] As Gillen d'Arcy Wood argues, Turner's depiction of the lake celebrated the tourist 'both intrepid and at play, circulating in a charmed intersection of adventure and leisure designed to appeal to the city-bound reader.'[17]

If illustration of the poem thus became more topographical in mode, and if, conversely, depictions of the topography were pervaded with the poem either explicitly or by implication, such a convergence of poem and the specificity of place was equally marked in other media. It is a feature, for example, of contemporary adaptations of the poem to the stage. In 1810, Thomas Dibdin's adaptation performing at the Surrey theatre opened and closed with a 'romantic view on Loch Katrine' and in between offered scenery depicting, for example, 'Another part of the mountain – the remains of a Gray horse lying among the underwood'.[18] By 1811, Edmund John Eyre's stage-adaptation for the Theatre Royal, Edinburgh, was boasting that 'The Scenery (Views from Nature) [was] taken on the spot'. To cite just two examples: Scene 1 opened with an overture accompanying a reveal of scenery described as: 'Loch Katrine—several islands, in perspective, scatter'd on the Lake with distant views of Ben-Venue and Ben A'an'; Act 2 opened with a grand set-piece: 'The Mountains—A Cataract, and rude Bridge thrown across a deep Glen.—[…]. By degrees, Day dawns.—The moment that the Sun appears above the most distant Mountain in the Perspective the Centinels blow their Horns, when RODERICK and his followers start up [from slumber]—Music expressive of the whole scene.'[19] This theatrical experience was delivering a quasi-touristic experience. Conversely, it was possible to promise a repetition of a remembered tourist experience to the theatre-goer. A typical playbill for the Royal Lyceum Theatre, Edinburgh, for another dramatisation, advertises the production to those who are already connoisseurs of the scenery: 'no Lover of the beautiful scenery of the Trossachs, around which Scott has cast such a halo of romance, should miss witnessing this magnificent production.' The playbill also promised a Panorama of Loch Katrine, and topographically accurate depictions of Coilantogle Ford and the Pass of Achray.[20]

That the realisation of the scenery of the poem in the theatre was connected to tourism is suggested by Joseph Pichot's account of his travels. Pichot fetched up in Edinburgh in the 1820s and divided his time between interviewing Scott at home about how best he might follow the itinerary of *The Lady of the Lake*, and attending a performance of *Rob Roy*. The scenery for this last was so realistic that he is inspired to remark that 'In fifteen days we shall be enabled, from the eminences of Ben Lomond, to command all the localities which the Lady of the Lake has rendered classical,' noting that 'these localities were conjured up where we sat [in the theatre], as if by magic.'[21]

Tourism to Loch Katrine was equally marked by a desire to superimpose the poem onto the place. This was achieved, for example, by re-mapping it. By 1813, the ever-opportunistic Ballantyne and Longman were advertising in the endpapers to *Rokeby* what must have been the first ever literary tourist map: described as 'a half-sheet map of the scenery of *The Lady of the Lake*', it was designed to slip into the pocket, and was accurate enough, the description suggests, for practical use, being 'taken from an actual survey and beautifully coloured'. In 1815, the French-American travel-writer Louis Simond also provided a sketch-map in his *Journal of a Tour and Residence in Great Britain, during the years 1810 and 1811* (1815). On this map the old names by which the locality was variously known before 1810, such as Loch Catheine, Loch Catherine, Loch Ketterin, Binean, and the Rough Island (a translation from the Gaelic) are showing signs of being replaced by names derived from *The Lady of the Lake* – Simond carefully marks the site of 'the Goblin's Cave' and the island as the 'island of the Lady of the Lake'.[22]

The re-mapping of the place by the poem was related to a sense that the tourist both could and should use the poem as a kind of guidebook to and dramatisation of the place, narrativising older pleasures of the picturesque. Simond's introductory remarks to his account of his day-excursion out from Callander on 7 September 1810 suggests how previous concepts of the picturesque are being expanded into the literary: 'We are just returned

from Loch Katrine [...]. We [...] have spent eight hours on a spot celebrated for its natural beauties, and still more now as the scene of the most
picturesque poem that ever was written' (I, 421). Subsequent comments
suggest that the beauties of the place were increasingly being imagined as
in part a reiteration or realisation of a previous reading experience: 'You
approach this consecrated spot with your imagination considerably exalted,
and prepared for something very wonderful' (I, 421). This impulse towards
the materialisation of text is supplemented by what Meisel might describe as
the impulse to 'illustration'. The experience of reading the poem is expanded
by additional information in the shape of the map provided and by verifica-
tion and identification of locations mentioned in the poem. Of particular
interest is Simond's desire, which Pichot would share some ten years later,
to measure the description offered in the poem against the actuality, an
impulse which leads to a series of mild disappointments: 'You approach this
consecrated spot with your imagination considerably exalted, and prepared
for something very wonderful. In this unfavourable state of mind, the first
sight of Loch Venachoir and Loch Achray did not satisfy us' (I, 421). Of
the island, to which they were rowed by a hired guide, he remarks that 'the
imagination of the poet has, if not embellished, at least much enlarged' it
(I, 422). The 'goblin-cave' he described as 'a mere dog-hole' (I, 423). But
Simond also records more satisfactory shocks of recognition: 'We knew at
first sight "The aged oak, That slanted from the islet rock."' He records, too,
practices commemorating such recognition: '[we] did not fail to gather a
few leaves and acorns, which will render us the object of envy among the
numerous readers of Mr Scott in America' (I, 422). He also mentions identi-
fying and viewing other locations that would become standard tourist-stops:
'Returning through the Trossachs [...] we remarked a narrow and wild pass
on the left, along the base of Ben-Ledi, which we pronounced to be the very
spot of the ambuscade of Roderick-Dhu; the whole scene between him and
Fitz-James was before us' (I, 424). As the examples above suggest, Simond's
account is threaded throughout with quotation from the poem, which has
the double effect of giving Scott's topographical descriptions of the place
documentary credibility and inlaying the place with the scenes of romance.

The many subsequent accounts of this excursion left by travellers
describe versions of Simond's efforts to re-experience the poem in situ. They
typically relate the ways in which tourists integrated their experience of
the poem with the landscape. Some had it by heart and recited it for the

benefit of fellow tourists; some had brought a copy borrowed from the piles thoughtfully provided at the hotel; some had merely brought a guidebook with the relevant stanzas extracted; some plotted the action on a map; some had it recited to them by the boatmen or guides.[23] Simond's sense of having the scene before him is reiterated over and over again as tourists enhanced the landscape by 'seeing' figures ambiguously remembered or imagined from the poem. So too is his sense of sharing the experience of realising the poem with other members of his party. Theodor Fontane, for example, remembered the game of quotations that his party played 'as a sort of conversational picnic'; less charming was the equally regular sense of defining the tourist's superior class and educational status as an under-standing of the fictive nature of Scott's romance, an understanding that the local Highland guides were often supposed not to share.[24] (Though the Scot John MacCulloch expresses quite a vindictive pleasure in the discomfiture of a too-credulous reader over the search for the Goblin's Cave: "'Lord, sir", said [the guide], "there is no cave here but what Mr Scott made himself." "What the d—l, no cave?" "Na, Sir, but we go where the gentry chooses, and they always ask for the goblin cave first."')[25]

One pleasure that Simond does not register, however, is the aural enhancement that was sometimes sought and provided. John Knox's painting 'Landscape with Tourists at Loch Katrine' (c.1820), in addition to depicting a number of well-dressed tourists and many of the amenities and activities I have already described (including the wicker picnic shelters, the viewing-stations, and a rowing-boat) includes the figure of a Highland piper. This man was almost certainly hired to provide an appropriate soundscape to the tourist experience, perhaps referencing the arrival of the Douglas and the singing of 'Hail to the chief'. There were other ways of providing a soundscape derived from the poem, too; MacCulloch remarks sourly on a Cockney sounding his horn in imitation of Fitz-James and in an effort to wake the same echoes; *Black's Guide* (1853) suggests enjoying the famous echo in the defile by whistling in imitation of Roderick Dhu.

Under pressure from the desire to re-experience the poem in situ, the place itself was slowly altered in other ways to correspond more closely with the poem. Hogg satirised this pandering to touristic desire for romance mercilessly; his Highlander supposedly tells him 'that Mr Burrel intended to build a bower in the lonely isle of Loch-Ketturin, in which he meant to place the prettiest girl that could be found in Edinburgh, during the summer months, to personate the Lady of the Lake; – that she was to be splendidly dressed in Highland Tartans, and ferry company over to the island; that Robert Maclean, a weaver at the Bridge of Turk, was to be the goblin of Correi-Uriskin [...]'[26] Yet nevertheless, not long after publication, Ellen's Isle did indeed boast a rustic shelter made to look like Ellen's bower as described in the poem, erected by the local landowners, Lord and Lady Willoughby d'Eresby. (This last was said to have been burned down by careless picnickers in 1837).[27] The whole experience was increasingly branded to Scott; whereas in the 1830s you might have embarked in the *Water Witch* and by 1843 in the steam-boat *The Gypsy*, by the late 1840s the boat had against convention switched sex. 1846 saw the launch of the steamer *Rob Roy*; *Rob Roy II* was launched in 1855; and the *Sir Walter Scott*, still running on the lake today, was launched on 31 October, 1899.

As the names of two of these steamers suggest, the longevity of literary tourism to Loch Katrine owed something to the ways in which Scott had subsequently populated the larger area with other characters and incidents featured in the Waverley novels. *The Lady of the Lake* was overlaid and supplemented by cultural memory of, in particular, *Waverley* (1814), *Old Mortality* (1816), and *Rob Roy* (1817). This produced a set of possible literary destinations and excursions increasingly linked through the concept of 'Scott country'. A tourist coming from the direction of Glasgow might start by visiting those sites in Glasgow associated with *Rob Roy*, such as the crypt of the cathedral, turn aside to examine others in Aberfoyle (notably the Bailie Nicol Jarvie inn and Jean McAlpine's inn), and, in travelling along Loch Ard, note the cliffs from which Helen Macgregor caused the unfortunate Morris to be thrown. Making his excursion out of Edinburgh, Pichot viewed in quick succession Stirling, Blacklin Falls outside Callander ('at length we could no longer doubt that we were traversing the same spots as Morton'), the 'MacGregor cave', and Katrine.[28] Whether commencing in Glasgow or Edinburgh, both itineraries tended to take in the view from the lake of the cave on the eastern shore of Loch Lomond, in which the historical Rob Roy supposedly hid; with the publication of the notes to the Magnum Opus edition, this cave was also identified as the one in which the kidnapped Edward Waverley is imprisoned.[29] *Vues Pittoresques* (1827) in part registers this elaboration of the original excursion by providing in addition to its two views of Loch Katrine a picture of the 'caverne de Rob-Roy' and another vignette of Loch Ard featuring Helen MacGregor.

The continuing importance of *The Lady of the Lake* to the Victorian idea of Scott in the 1870s can be measured in part by the size and importance of the statue of Ellen Douglas standing on the lowest tier of the Scott monument in Edinburgh. One of the larger figures, it was also one of the earliest installed. In the early 1900s, it was still eminently possible to visit Loch Katrine with a view to re-experiencing Scott's poem. Sir George Biddell Airy, in preparing his 1904 edition of the poem, supplied it with fifty full-page photographs of locations specified in the poem, 'A Topography of the Poem', and a formidable map referencing all the events of the poem to the Ordnance Survey. In so doing, he aimed to make it possible for the reader accurately to retrace the author's own reconstruction of the journeys of Fitz-James and Roderick Dhu. The magic was still potent for Airy: 'in terminating the notes on this beautiful poem, I remark that the accuracy of Scott's topography gives a mental reality to the incidents, and the pleasure of examining them on the spot, such as I have never experienced in reference to any other literature'.[30] A Caledonian Railway brochure of 1907 which promoted the trip to the Highlands with a picture of Ellen in her boat also provides evidence that in the early 1900s the desire to 'follow the course of the chase as described in Scott's *Lady of the Lake*' remained compelling enough to be commercially profitable. But, by the 1920s, the visual record suggests that Scott's hold on this landscape was in decay. A hundred years later the pleasurable bustle of Knox's painting has given way to a series of severer depictions of Loch Katrine as a relatively deserted place, frequented by cattle or at most, fishermen, and this seems to have been the case whether in fine art, promotional posters, or souvenir postcards.[31]

The decay of literary tourism inspired by *The Lady of the Lake* was bound up with the general decline in Scott's hold on national and international culture by the 1920s. It is acknowledged in the valedictory remarks of the editor of one 1927 school textbook of extracts from the poem, *Scott's Narrative Poetry, Being Abridgements of The Lay of the Last Minstrel, Marmion, and The Lady of the Lake*. Amongst pages of possible assignments, the author, A. J. J. Ratcliffe, suggests this one: 'Write a letter as from a hotel in the Trossachs, sketching the kind of country round you. Draw a map in illustration, and say how the place has changed since the days of Roderick Dhu'.[32] The end of Scott's deep imbrication in national and anglophone culture, however, is hinted at in the accompanying valedictory and defiant remark that, although 'it is alleged that Scott is unpopular with young people', this merely made it all the more necessary and desirable for a competent teacher to make sure that the poem was read.[33] Here, it is perhaps possible to pinpoint the very moment when the promised indulgences of holiday romance are fatally overtaken by educational conscientiousness. Ratcliffe's Junior and Middle School pupils may well have been the first to refuse to pursue Scott tourism beyond slogging through that particular holiday task. At the bicentenary of the publication of *The Lady of the Lake*, it has been left to scholars to try to replicate the freshness of the experience of two hundred years ago, experimentally reinvigorating the landscape with our collective memory of the lines of Scott.

Notes

1 James Hogg, 'Highland Adventures', in *Winter Evening Tales, collected among the cottagers in the south of Scotland* 2nd edn. (Edinburgh: Oliver and Boyd, 1821), 2 vols.: vol. 1, p. 144. This chapter draws upon and extends earlier work published in Nicola J. Watson, *The Literary Tourist: Readers and Places in Romantic and Victorian Britain* (Basingstoke: Palgrave Macmillan, 2006), and in the *Bulletin of the Edinburgh Sir Walter Scott Club* (2010) as part of the colloquium celebrating the bicentenary of the publication of *The Lady of the Lake*.

2 James Hogg, 'Highland Adventures', in *Winter Evening Tales*, I, p. 147.

3 Charles Roger, *A Week at Bridge of Allan [...]* (1851) 3rd edn. enlarged (Edinburgh: Adam and Charles Black, 1853), p. 282.

4 Dorothy Wordsworth, *Recollections of a Tour Made in Scotland in 1803* in *The Journals of Dorothy Wordsworth*, ed. Ernest de Selincourt, 2 vols. (London: Macmillan, 1941), vol. I, p. 271.

5 In 1853, Charles Roger suggested that the first person who drove to the Trossachs was the countess of Hyndford, in 1799, but this is unlikely to be true. Roger, *A Week at Bridge of Allan*, p. 282.

6 For more detail on contemporary commentary on the area before the publication of *The Lady of the Lake*, see the chapters by Tom Furniss, Dorothy McMillan and Michael Newton in this volume.

7 Patrick Graham, *Sketches Descriptive of Picturesque Scenery, on the southern confines of Perthshire* (Edinburgh: for Peter Hill and W. Hunter, 1806), p. 16.

8 Graham, p. 28; for details of Dr Lucas' diary for August 1810, comments by Mrs Grant of Laggan and John Sinclair, see Alastair Durie's chapter in this volume; Elizabeth Isabella Spence, *Sketches of the manners, customs and scenery of Scotland* (London: Longmans, 1811), vol. I, p. 200.

9 For a version of this point, see James Holloway and Lindsay Errington, *The Discovery of Scotland: The Appreciation of Scottish Scenery through Two Centuries of Painting* (Edinburgh: National Gallery of Scotland, 1978), p. 109.

10 In, for example, her paper at the ASLS conference, 'Scott, the Trossachs and the Tourists', Balloch, 5–6 June 2010.

11 *The Lady of the Lake. A Poem by Walter Scott Esq. Illustrated with engravings from paintings by Richard Cook with engravings from the designs of Richard Westall* (Edinburgh, 1811; London: John Sharpe, 1811), Canto 3rd, Note X, p. lxiii.

12 On this see Watson (2006), pp. 132–50.
13 Martin Meisel, *Realizations: Narrative, Pictorial, and Theatrical Arts in Nineteenth-century England* (Princeton: Princeton University Press, 1983), p. 30.
14 John Martin, *Illustrations; Landscape, Historical, and Antiquarian to the Poetical Works of Sir Walter Scott, Bart.* (London: Tilt, 1834), vol. XIII, pp. 39, 54, 295.
15 There would be many later representations of Loch Katrine which had at their heart *The Lady of the Lake*, such as Horatio McCulloch's 'Loch Katrine' (1866). For a discussion of this painting as a representation of 'a landscape that is central to the history of Scottish tourism', marking it as a hidden, romantic world, see John Glendening, *The High Road: Romantic Tourism, Scotland, and Literature 1720–1820* (Basingstoke: Palgrave Macmillan, 1997), p. 234.
16 J. M. W. Turner's documentary landscape illustration to Cadell's edition of the complete *Poetical Works* (1833) 'Each volume to have a Frontispiece and Vignette title-page from designs taken from real scenes by J. W. Turner, R.A.'
17 Gillen d'Arcy Wood, 'Working Holiday: Turner as Waverley Tourist', *The Wordsworth Circle* 31: 2 (Spring 2000), pp. 83–8; p. 87.
18 Thomas John Dibdin, *The Lady of the Lake; a melo-dramatic romance in two acts (from Sir Walter Scott) printed from the Acting Copy [...]* (Dublin: J. Charles, [1810]).
19 Edmund John Eyre, *The Lady of the Lake: A Melodramatic Romance in three acts; taken from the popular poem of that title, and now performing with undiminished applause at the Theatre Royal, Edinburgh* (London: for W. H. Wyatt, 1811).
20 Scottish Theatre Archive, Glasgow Special Collections.
21 Joseph Jean M. C. Amédée Pichot, *Historical and Literary Tour of a Foreigner in England and Scotland*, 2 vols. (London: Saunders and Otley, 1825), p. 335.
22 Louis Simond, *Journal of a Tour and Residence in Great Britain, during the years 1810 and 1811* (1815) 2 vols. (2nd ed. Edinburgh: Constable, 1817) vol. I, p. 423.
23 For further details, see Watson (2006), pp. 160–2.
24 Theodore Fontane, *Across the Tweed: A Tour of Mid-Victorian Scotland*, tr. Brian Battershaw, intro. Sir James Fergusson (London: Phoenix House, 1965), p. 104.
25 John MacCulloch, *The Highlands and Western Islands of Scotland, Containing Descriptions of their Scenery and Antiquities [...] Founded as a Series of Annual Journeys between the years 1811 and 1821, and forming a universal guide to that country, in Letters to Sir Walter Scott, Bart*, 4 vols. (London: Longman et al., 1824), vol. I, p. 165.
26 Hogg, vol. I, p. 144–5.
27 See Roger, p. 328, amongst others, for a mention of this structure, noting that 'its removal or destruction is certainly a cause of regret.'
28 Pichot, pp. 468–483.
29 Charles Macready, for example, supplemented his tour of Loch Katrine with a jaunt to Rob Roy's cave as early as 1818. See Charles Macready, *Macready's Reminiscences, and Selections from his Diaries and Letters*, ed. Sir Frederick Pollock, 2 vols. (London: Macmillan & Co., 1875), vol. I, p. 141.
30 George Biddell Airy, *The Lady of the Lake* (London: A. & C. Black, 1904), p. 154.
31 Railway poster, 1925; see also depictions by Sidney Richard Percy (1821–1886), William Mellor (1851–1931), and Francis Jamieson (1895–1950).
32 A. J. J. Ratcliffe, *Scott's Narrative Poetry, Being Abridgements of The Lay of the Last Minstrel, Marmion, and The Lady of the Lake* (London and Edinburgh: Nelson, 1927), p. 252.
33 Ratcliffe, p. 253.

Wildness and wet: artistic interactions and the Trossachs' designation as a National Park

JIM ALISON

This morning I left Stirling and went to Callander, thence to Inversnaid by coach and boat, by the Trossachs and Loch Katrine, thence through Loch Lomond and the mountains to a railroad and on to this charming Oban. I have just arrived this day on Lochs Katrine and Lomond and the drives through the passes and over the mountains made famous by Scott in *The Lady of the Lake* will be long remembered – 'Ower the muir amang the heather'. The heather is just coming into bloom and it is glorious. Wish I could camp in it for a month. All the scenery is interesting, but nothing like Alaska or California in grandeur. (John Muir, in a letter to his wife Louie, 1893)[1]

Just over a hundred years ago, in summer 1906, the Scots-born John Muir successfully lobbied the US Congress to place California's Yosemite Park under Federal protection. The Scottish Parliament was similarly motivated to create Scotland's first National Park. Designated 'Loch Lomond and the Trossachs' in July 2002, it covers some 1,800 square kilometres from Balloch in the south to Tyndrum, from St Fillans in the east to Glenbranter in the west. Among the potentially conflicting duties laid upon the Park Authority, the priority is to 'conserve and enhance' the region's cultural heritage.[2] Focusing on one small aspect of this remit, this chapter considers what some visiting writers and artists made of their expectations and experiences within the territory of the Trossachs in the century between roughly 1785 and 1885.

'The Trossachs are often visited by persons of taste, who are desirous of seeing nature in her rudest and most unpolished state.' So said Dr Robertson, parish minister of Callander in 1791 in the *First Statistical Account of Scotland*.[3] The etymology of the Gaelic place-name is obscure: possibly 'rough ground' or 'crossing'. Either would fit. In the narrow sense, and it really is narrow, the location is the short, densely wooded pass leading from Loch Katrine to Loch Achray, which Walter Scott called the 'romantic avenue'. James Hogg, who walked through in 1803, suggested to him that its chaotic form might have its genesis in Noah's Flood.[4] More broadly, the lie of the land, defined by three chains of lochs running mainly from west to east, has been forged by the geology of the Highland Boundary fault cutting through Balmaha, Aberfoyle and Callander, and demarcating highland from lowland, culturally as well as geographically. It also passed through the imagination of Walter Scott. One need only go up to the Visitors' Centre on the Duke's Pass to sense that things cracked and shifted around here. On the scale of California's San Andreas fault the area is no great shakes perhaps, but it is still tremulous, triggering occasional headlines such as 'Earthquake tremors rock the Trossachs', and 'Trossachs village struck by fresh earthquakes'.[5]

Moreover the area's climate has always been moist: its annual rainfall is twice the UK's average. Dr Patrick Graham, another *Statistical* minister, writes in his account of Aberfoyle: 'In this neighbourhood fevers are the most frequent diseases; they are to be attributed to the natives being much exposed to getting wet, in a climate where from the mountainous nature of the country, rains are frequent.'[6] Graham, clearly a graduate of the Enlightenment, goes on, like Hogg, to mix theology and hydrology, speculating on 'the real effects that are to be attributed to running water, that universal agent, as some modern philosophers account it, in changing the superficial aspect of our earth'.[7] Not surprisingly the wider Trossachs became the catchment for much of the water supply of the Scottish midlands, and in the course of 150 years of massive engineering its romantic landmarks have been degraded. It is ironic that when Victoria and Albert visited Loch Katrine in 1859 to inaugurate Glasgow's splendid new water system they were disappointed to find that it was raining.

Until well after the 1745 Rising this zone was sparsely peopled, seen as the wild frontier. The few routes were droving tracks or military roads. To Lowlanders, however unjustly in the perspective offered by Michael Newton's chapter, these badlands were frequented by cattle thieves, smugglers and outlaws who spoke their own 'Erse' language, suspected by its non-Gaelic-speaking neighbours. On its eastern border, Menteith, the Trossachs had always been moated by the great barrier of the River Forth marshes though Lord Kames, Enlightenment luminary and 'gentleman farmer', was helping to open it up by draining the bogs of the Flanders Moss. Robert Burns, on the western fringes in summer 1787, noted, with emphatic distaste, 'A country where savage streams tumble over savage mountains, thinly overspread with savage flocks, which starvingly support as savage inhabitants'.[8] For Robert Kirk, the scholarly seventeenth-century minister of Aberfoyle, this landscape had also, however, sheltered an occult parallel world of which he gave his own ethnographic account which he called *The Secret Commonwealth.*[9]

The conception of the area as somehow wild in nature and lawless in its society remained. That most notorious of the Lowlanders' perceived 'Highland Rogues', Robert MacGregor – Rob Roy – had died in 1734, but as late as 1788, when the law tried to serve a writ on an unruly family of McLarens in the remoter reaches of Balquhidder, it was deemed prudent that there should be an armed escort. As a result, a lame youngster of 17 found himself riding out with a troop of redcoats from Stirling over the hills to Invernenty. By the time he got there the culprits had cannily made themselves scarce.[10] That young man was a raw legal apprentice, then called Wattie Scott, who never forgot his first jaunt into the Trossachs. The melodramatic 'Glenfinlas; or, Lord Ronald's Coronach', his first acknowledged poem, is set in the area and, as a gruesome tale of spectral seduction, distorts local folklore through a fashionable German lens. Subsequently, exploiting his contacts with local gentry, he came to know the area well. Despite his limp, the young Scott was an enterprising walker and horseman. His later writing on the area appears to be based in substantial intimate local knowledge.

In 1803 this same terrain around Loch Katrine and Balquhidder saw the eccentric arrival of three great English writers. William Wordsworth, Samuel Coleridge, and Wordsworth's sister Dorothy were undertaking a tour of the Highlands in late summer. The ostensible reason for the trip was health and, although at times only Dorothy seemed fit, all proved tough pedestrians. They spent three wet August days splashing around the lochsides until Coleridge became so miserable in the rain that they agreed that he should break away on his own. Dorothy's journal at that point worried about 'poor Coleridge'.[11] Coleridge's jottings on the other hand conceal in Latin a heartfelt good riddance, 'utinam nonq. vidissem' ('I wish I had never seen', adapted from Cicero's *Letters to Atticus*).[12] The Lakers were waterfall fanciers. They were moved by images and sounds of cascading water and the whole aesthetic of cataracts, linked to notions of the picturesque and the sublime. Of course, they had no shortage of these in the Trossachs. All three in their different ways wrote lyrically of meeting a fourteen-year-old Highland girl at the waterfall of Inversnaid, the sister of the ferryman. While Dorothy conveyed the happy innocence of the encounter as she changed out of her sodden clothes, William produced a yearning, slightly creepy poem, 'To a Highland Girl at Inversneyde'. Meanwhile, Coleridge noted 'Now the fall was in all its fury [...] we stayed all day in the comfortless hovel, comfortless, but the two little lasses did every thing with *such sweetness*, and one of them, 14, with such native elegance. O she was a divine creature!'[13] Later, in the autumn at the end of an extended tour, the Wordsworths headed south in their ramshackle jaunting car. A few days later they were welcomed by that other up-and-coming writer, Walter Scott, by then the Shirra of Selkirk. To their delight, he read them work in progress, a rhyming narrative entitled *The Lay of the Last Minstrel*, about border feuding.

After the success of *The Lay* and *Marmion*, Scott turned to the Trossachs as a frontier locale for a third verse tale, and made return visits to collect local colour. This work emerged in 1810 as *The Lady of The Lake*.[14] The poem's *mise-en-scène* is less well-known than once it was. The year is 1530. One fine day King James V, disguised as Fitz-James, a knight from the court at Stirling, is hounding a stag in the glens around Loch Achray. At dusk he finds himself bewildered in the Trossachs defile. Sheltered overnight by the beautiful Ellen Douglas on an island on Loch Katrine, he plans to make her his mistress and the romantic tale unfolds from this opening situation. It is exuberantly glamourised, the landscape as well as the history. Nonetheless, the poem has an important serious theme, the clash in the border zone of two ways of life, and, in Scott's view, the 'inevitable' defeat of the older, more 'primitive' Celtic culture. While Michael Newton's chapter rightly takes issue with such a worldview and cultural stance, Scott, the anglophone Lowlander writing at the beginning of the nineteenth century, was engaged by existing conceptions, which he enhanced, of the Trossachs – and the Gàidhealtachd in general – as 'wild'. Within this imaginary framework, Scott was lavish with his special effects: picturesque vistas alternate with songs and action sequences including the hunt, the voyage of the chief's galley and the sending of the fiery cross. There had been nothing in English poetry quite like that atmospheric first canto.

The *Lady* was an unprecedented bestseller, although, overall, the work has often seemed less appealing to contemporary tastes. Its 4,500 tetrameter lines can be read as settling into a hypnotic trot, which Coleridge, not alone, found nearly unreadable.[15] Nonetheless, Ian Brown has suggested that part of the reason for its public success in its time may lie in that very dynamic rhythm and the skill, in some sense performative and calling for the spoken voice, with which Scott manages his changes and variations of rhythm. Further the poem's overall rhythmic impetus is modified and complemented by Scott's use of intermittent intervening poems, which, like 'The Coronach', have a free-standing power, yet also operate within the overall architectonics of the poem – in Brown's view as a playwright, its dramaturgy – rather as arias in opera or songs in a modern musical. They are choric as Shakespeare's songs often are in his plays, but also take forward the action. In Brown's interpretation, the steady, though subtly modulated, rhythms allow Scott to achieve remarkable dramatic effects in his poem.[16] As David Manderson observes in his chapter in this volume, Scott often achieves effects which we would now describe as 'filmic'. Robert Cadell the publisher recalled that:

> The whole country rang with praises of the poet [...] crowds set off to view the scenery of Loch Katrine, till then comparatively unknown; and as the book came out just before the season for excursions, every house and inn in that neighbourhood was crammed with a constant succession of visitors.[17]

This reaction is hardly surprising given the poem's formula as well as what has just been observed about its poetics and framing of its action. It is a tale of one summer week: six cantos, each a day from dawn to dusk in an exotic landscape – and without a drop of Trossachs rain. The poem idealises the country in which it is set and becomes an ideal promotion for the infant Highland holiday trade. The better class of hostelry furnished its guests with copies to serve as guide books.

The poem came to have additional resonances in the nineteenth century. Artists carted their sketch books, and their umbrellas, to the east end of Loch Katrine. In 1819 Rossini composed his opera *La Donna del Lago* for San Carlo, with the MacGregors transformed into Neapolitan partisans, and by 1830 there were twenty different translations of the poem into European languages. It is fascinating that after 1859 *The Lady of the Lake* began to be seen allegorically as the patron deity of the Glasgow–Loch Katrine water system. In the city's Kelvingrove Park there still towers an ornate commemorative fountain topped by a heroic bronze of Ellen, an angel of public health. Paradoxically, she also perches demurely with her paddle on the facade of the former headquarters of the whisky company which produced the popular blend *Roderick Dhu*.[18] Further, *The Lady* was apparently the favourite poem of Queen Victoria, who held thirty-two copies at Balmoral.[19]

Victoria also cherished twelve copies of *Rob Roy* (1817), another work of Scott's whose action, at least in significant part, impinges on the Trossachs region. Prefacing a later edition, Scott makes clear that he regards this novel, some of whose implications are discussed at greater length by David Hewitt in the next chapter, as his 'Highland Fault' manifesto, underlining again the trope of the Highlands as 'wild'. Of Rob he says:

> It is this strong contrast betwixt the civilised and cultivated mode of life on one side of the Highland line and the wild and lawless adventures which were habitually undertaken and achieved by one who dwelled on the opposite side of that ideal boundary which creates the interest attached to his name.[20]

In 1715, with rebellion stirring, in the latter part of the novel its English hero, young Frank Osbaldistone, 'does the Trossachs' in a hectic three days. It seems a late summer sortie in fine harvest weather – again not a drop of rain. The only ones to get wet are Morris the spy, drowned in Loch Ard by order of Rob's wife, the fearsome Helen; and Rob himself who escapes under water when his captors are fording the Forth. Though rain never dampened Scott's representations of the Trossachs, he was, like the English romantics, fascinated by waterfalls. In one memorable exchange with Nicol Jarvie, the Glasgow merchant, Helen MacGregor describes herself as an impetuous natural force like a Highland torrent; and later the MacGregors stage a clan gathering in the amphitheatre of a cataract which is meant to impress the Sassenach. This fall at Ledard, which Scott had himself visited, features in two of his novels. In *Waverley* the picturesque, feminine aspect of the three-stage cascade is emphasised, its surrounds having been planted out by Flora MacIvor with shrubs that 'added to the grace without diminishing the romantic wildness of the scene'.[21] In *Rob Roy*, however, the mood is more awe-inspiring than pretty. In the aesthetics of the time it is sublime. Again Scott's work was an immediate best-seller and has had an after-life, which it has never entirely lost. From the entertaining business of Isaack Pocock's musical romp *Rob Roy; or, Auld Langsyne, an Operatic Drama in Three Acts* (1818)[22], which has a plausible claim to be the dormant seed from

which Scotland's new National Theatre has finally germinated, as Barbara
Bell's work on the nineteenth-century National Drama makes clear,[23] to
Alan Sharp's lively screenplay for the 1995 film starring Liam Neeson and
Jessica Lange, Scott's novel continues to inspire many dramatic and filmic
adaptations. Moreover, for those so inclined, there also exist *Bailie Nicol
Jarvie, Rob Roy* and *Clan MacGregor* whiskies.

Before Scott emerged, the influential literary stimuli for tourists had
been the *Ossian* poems and travelogues such as those of Pennant, Dr
Johnson, and Gilpin. The Trossachs had been merely an occasional digres-
sion between the Falls of Clyde and Fingal's Cave. Looking back, Scott
modestly conceded that his work in *Rob Roy* and *The Lady of the Lake* might
have done a little to popularise them, but after his death his old friend
and political opponent the Whig lawyer Lord Cockburn made a much
grander claim: 'His genius immortalises the region.'[24] But Cockburn also
knew from firsthand experience that Scott's representations had created a
beguiling Trossachs of the mind far from the landscape and experiences
that travellers would encounter on the ground. Certainly, Cockburn and
his friend Francis Jeffrey were nostalgic ruralists who affected like Horace
to 'cultivate literature on a little oatmeal', weekending in their reconstituted
towerhouses at Bonaly and Craigcrook on the hilly fringes of Edinburgh.
Cockburn even had his own secluded waterfall which he invoked in a sentimental poem called 'The Linn':

> How purely thy rill from its old rocks descends;
> Amusing the air by its breeze-varied sound!
> And fixing the eye on the arches it bends
> Unheeding the wildness that watches around.[25]

Yet, while Jeffrey and Cockburn were both lovers of the Loch Lomond
and Trossachs region, they confronted its climatic limitations more real-
istically than Scott ever did. Jeffrey the founding editor of the *Edinburgh
Review*, who could be a supercilious critic, is at his most endearing as a
family man who summered loyally at Stuckgowan, a lovely Georgian gothic
villa on the shores of Loch Lomond, and made a virtue of its persistent
rain. He is probably the first of many Scots to suggest that getting soaked
is an essential detoxifying ingredient of the annual holiday. Writing to his
American father-in-law in 1822 he boasts:

It rained almost every day while we were in the Highlands, and most commonly all day; but the weather never confined Charlotte or me for an hour, and I do not think at all interfered with our enjoyment. It was soft and calm and balmy, and we walked and rowed and climbed and scrambled, without minding the rain any more than the ravens. We were out eight or nine hours every day, thoroughly wet most of the time, and never experienced the least inconvenience or discomfort; but came home more plump and rosy than we had been since last year. The roaring of the mountain torrents in a calm morning after a raining night has something quite delicious to my ears [...].[26]

Cockburn's *Circuit Journeys* are witty, indiscreet jottings of his travels, often with his congenial family entourage, as an old-style circuit judge. The journeys are part work, and part holiday. Quite how he justified the official expenses of three different trips to Loch Katrine in the course of his legal duties is another matter! Here he is, in 1837, encountering at first hand the disconcerting impact of his friend Scott on accommodation in the Trossachs:

The inn near the Trossachs could, perhaps, put up a dozen, or at the very most, two dozen people; but last autumn I saw about one hundred apply for admittance, and after horrid altercations, entreaties, and efforts, about fifty or sixty were compelled to huddle together all night. They were all of the upper rank, travelling mostly in private carriages, and by far the greater number strangers. But the pigs were as comfortably accommodated. I saw three or four English *gentlemen* spreading their own straw on the earthen floor of an outhouse, with a sparred door, and no fire-place or furniture. And such things occur every day here, though the ground belongs to a duke and partly to an earl [...].[27]

On the topic of living like pigs, we have a glimpse of artists attempting to survive in the wilds. In July 1853 there arrived at Glenfinglas the philosopher John Ruskin, his Scots wife Effie, and John Everett Millais, a young pre-Raphaelite. The trio had rented a cottage by the burnside at Brig o' Turk for a working holiday. Ruskin was preparing lectures for publication,

while Millais was tackling a landscape portrait of Ruskin. As with the
Wordsworths and Coleridge fifty years earlier, this was a *ménage a trois*
bringing north the baggage of its own complicated relationships. Their
project also ran into trouble, and roughing it in rain and primitive accommodation did not help. Ruskin, fascinated by the rock strata of the Finglas
waterfalls, reports to his father in London:

> Millais has fixed on his place, a lovely piece of worn rock, with
> foaming water and weeds and moss, and a noble overhanging bank
> of dark crag; and I am to be standing looking quietly down the
> stream [...] we shall have two of the most wonderful torrents in the
> world, Turner's St Gothard and Millais' Glenfinlas.[28]

Unfortunately the weather was foul, they were tormented by midges and
their domestic arrangements proved embarrassingly cramped. Effie writes
confidingly to her mother:

> Crawley thinks Mrs Ruskin would be awfully horrified if she saw
> our dwelling. John, Millais and I have each two little dens where we
> have room to sleep and turn but no place whatever to put anything
> in, there being no drawers, but I have established a file of nails from
> which my clothes hang, and John sleeps on the sofa in the parlour.[29]

Ruskin toiled away, unaware that intimacy between Effie and Millais
was growing. The tensions are, however, lurking in Millais' two remarkable paintings of the Finglas falls. In his portrait, Ruskin, dressed in black,
postures in the ravine of a white-water cascade. In the other – more warmly
coloured – work, titled 'The Waterfall', Effie in bonnet and shawl sits
doucely sewing in middle distance, on a rock shelf beside the burn. You do
not, of course, see the artist, the third party. As things shortly turned out, it
was the Ruskin marriage that was on the rocks, divorce resulted, and Effie
and Millais married in 1855.

The commercial opening of the Trossachs to domestic and foreign
visitors brought not only more seemly sleeping quarters, but also improved
amenities of all kinds. Among these were the guide books. Their most
notable forerunner had been Sarah Murray's no-nonsense commentary *The
Beauties of Scotland*, published in 1797. A gutsy Kensington widow in her

fifties, to whom earlier chapters have referred, she covered, travelling by chaise with one servant, some 2,000 miles, taking in 'everything worth seeing'. She reveals the same shrewd eye as her contemporary Dorothy Wordsworth. Her adventures included characteristically vigorous struggles with Trossachs and Loch Lomond weather: 'It was impossible to be more wet and dirty than I was.'[30]

In 1810, exploiting the success of *The Lady of the Lake*, Scott's friend Patrick Graham, the minister of Aberfoyle, augmented his previous *Statistical Account* into the first general guidebook to the area.[31] As well as instruction on how to read landscapes aesthetically, and comments on soil, climate and the character of the inhabitants, it describes the *Daoine Shih*. These shadowy, disgruntled 'Men of Peace' are the same Elves and Fauns who populate his predecessor's *Secret Commonwealth*. One later, more specialised local guide first appeared in 1851. This is *A Week at Bridge of Allan* […]. The work of Charles Roger, a local minister, song collector and entrepreneur who championed the cause of the National Wallace Monument, *A Week* is a thoroughly obsequious promotion of the Spa above all its English and continental rivals. But there is much of interest even today in the suggested itineraries which steer genteel excursionists into the heart of Scott country. Roger's Trossachs chapters start from an assumption: 'To this land of mountain and flood, for many years *The Lady of the Lake* served as the only guide, and, with whatever accessory, it is still the tourist's best companion.'[32] His commentary highlights the romantic theme, and tends to work to one formula: a piece of historical or topographical detail is illustrated by a quotation from Scott's poem, followed by obeisance to the local laird and a puff for an adjacent hotel.

Among the troops of visitors taking in the Trossachs Tour, guide books in hand, were assorted writers, artists and musicians. Three distinguished European birds of passage have been rediscovered through recent translations of their Scottish experiences. Krystyn Lach-Szyrma's *Reminiscences of a Journey through Scotland, 1820–1824* were rendered from Polish in 1941 but published only in 2004. Lach-Szyrma had arrived in Edinburgh, aged 22, as tutor to three princes of the elite Polish Czartoryski clan. Having entrée to the best circles he coolly observed notables such as Scott, Cockburn, Jeffrey and Hogg. He took in the Trossachs during an energetic excursion whose main goal was the island of Staffa. Here he nearly drowned swimming into Fingal's Cave. His exploits include a sodden ascent of Ben Lomond.

On returning to base camp in Tarbet he and his companions spent the evening declaiming passages from Hogg's *The Queen's Wake*, after which they affirmed with perhaps tipsy solemnity that 'Only then when we had seen reality and compared it with the description did we realise how great the difference is between life and art. They are separated by a sort of gulf which increases or diminishes according to the genius of the poet'.[33] In 1858, Theodor Fontane was a young Prussian press attaché making his first pilgrimage. He was an enthusiastic reader of Scott, 'My favourite poet, still more my favourite human being', and later he was to emerge as one of Germany's finest novelists, the author of *Effie Briest*. His travelogue *Beyond the Tweed* is an affectionately ironic account for German readers of a journey north, starting like Lach-Szyrma's in Edinburgh, taking in battlefields, castles, sights such as Staffa and Iona, but culminating in his personal Mecca of Abbotsford. He describes the bog-standard day-trip, with Pickwickian echoes, on an overloaded coach from a Stirling hotel across to the Trossachs, on by steamboat to Stronachlachar and back to Stirling in the sunset. Amusedly he records the naïve commercialism and the difference between legend and reality on the Trossachs trail – incorporating a prose crib of the plot of *The Lady of the Lake* – very useful if like Coleridge, you feel that you will never make it to the end of the original.[34] A year later Jules Verne, Scott-worshipping and hyperactive, made a rapid, zigzag transit. Parts of his account, later published as *'Backwards to Britain'*, he also worked into *Les Indes noires*, now translated as *The Underground City*.[35] This concerns a coal-mining community living on the shores of the fantastical subterranean Loch Malcolm under the Trossachs (named presumably in honour of Scott's juvenile lead in *The Lady of the Lake*) and is discussed in detail in Ian Thompson's chapter in this volume. In its climax an aged villain pulls the plug on Loch Katrine, which spills its contents into the caverns below, though all ends happily with a colliers' wedding underground. In his own bizarre way, Verne, like Robert Kirk describing the haunts and cavities of the elves, seems to sense that there may be more to this region than meets the rational eye.

Other literary tourists, native and foreign, have left brief but revealing records of their excursions, including Washington Irving, Thomas Carlyle, Robert Southey, Hans Christian Andersen, Alexander Smith, Nathaniel Hawthorne, Queen Victoria, William Topaz McGonagall, and many more. There were also artists, some discussed in detail by Murdo Macdonald in his chapter: Turner, the panorama painters Nasmyth, Knox, McCulloch and Bough, and the pioneering photographer Fox Talbot creating his 'sun pictures'. Then in October 1881, again at Brig o' Turk, the *Glasgow Boys* arrived *en plein air*, generating among other pieces, the young James Guthrie's brooding *A Funeral Service in the Highlands*, where the coffin in the snow is that of a village lad drowned in the waters of the Finglas burn.[36]

Finally that same autumn, over at Inversnaid, one of the world's favourite poems came to be written. Gerard Hopkins had been drafted as a temporary curate to a poor Glasgow parish, which was proving to be very hard going. On a day off, he took a steamboat trip on Loch Lomond, and found himself briefly by the verge of the Inversnaid waterfall in lowering, supersaturated weather. His letters suggest that he had read Wordsworth's *Highland Girl*, but *Inversnaid* is certainly not emotion recollected in tranquillity. The intense sights and sounds of the cascade; that hint of dark despair; the final prayer for wildness and wet which has become a conservation mantra – these seem powerfully immediate reactions. If you visit the fall today, you realise that his plea went unnoticed: the flow was later diminished by the Arklet dam built for Glasgow's waterworks. Graham, the eighteenth-century minister of Aberfoyle, had seen the power of water as the 'universal agent'. A century later, the Jesuit Hopkins sensed that it was the living *instress* of the natural world and signified the presence of God. Its absence meant desiccation of all that is creative. Hopkins' later career was tragic. Leaving Glasgow he latterly taught classics in Dublin. Punitive feelings of inadequacy deepened into the depression from which issued his last 'Terrible Sonnets'. In one of these he prays:

> [...] birds build—but not I build; no, but strain,
> Time's eunuch, and not breed one work that wakes:
> Mine, o thou lord of life, send my roots rain.[37]

'Send my roots rain': Hopkins died a few weeks after these words, aged forty-four. He had contracted typhoid fever – ironically, from Dublin's polluted public water supply.

This chapter started in 1791 with Dr Robertson's 'nature in her rudest and most unpolished state' and we end in 1881 with 'wildness and wet', not so much a progression as variations on a persisting theme. Lowland Scots has a graphic adjective, *clarty*, which conveys muddiness and filth. The reader will recall that after the success of *The Lady of the Lake* Scott bought a rundown farm called 'Clarty Hole' and began to transform it into his grandiose dream, 'Abbotsford'. The chapter has offered examples of the ways writers and artists, whether consciously or not, have put Scott's exotic vision of the Trossachs to the test of their own often clarty experiences underfoot. One may speculate whether any other region of Scotland documents so vividly the interrelationships, aesthetic, psychological and commercial between representation and reality. This brief survey has also dealt with the accumulation of only a century of cultural responses to a changing landscape. Yet it is surely true that it is the accumulation of such responses, interrelating landscape and imagination over several centuries, but much enhanced by the impact of Walter Scott's imaginative writing that has led to the designation of Loch Lomond and the Trossachs as a National Park. This accumulation of creative responses continues and amounts to a complex imaginative asset for the Park, and for the larger community that enjoys it.[38]

Notes

1   Letter dated Station Hotel Oban, July 22 1893, digitised in *John Muir Correspondence*, Holt-Atherton Special Collections, University of the Pacific, Stockton, California.
2   Four statutory aims are stated in Section 1 of the National Parks (Scotland) Act 2000 (asp 10), TSO (the Stationery Office) 2000.
3   James Robertson, 'Parish of Callander' in *The Statistical Account of Scotland (1791–1799)*, vol. 11, p. 576.
4   James Hogg, letter to Walter Scott dated Glen Gyle, 29 May 1803, *James Hogg's Highland Tours*, ed. W. F. Lauchlan (Hawick: Byway Books, 1981), p. 51.
5   Items in *The Sunday Herald*, 21 and 28 June 2003.
6   Patrick Graham, 'Parish of Aberfoyle' in *The Statistical Account of Scotland (1791–1799)*, vol. 10, p. 120.
7   Ibid., p. 116.
8   Robert Burns, letter to Robert Ainslie, dated Arrochar, 25 June 1787, in *The Letters of Robert Burns*, ed. G. Ross Roy (Oxford: Oxford University Press, 1985), vol. 1, p. 124.
9   Robert Kirk, *The Secret Common-Wealth an Essay of the Nature and actions of the Subterranean and (for the most part) Invisible people heiretoforgoing under the names of ELVES, FAUNES and FAIRIES* [...] in Michael Hunter, *The Occult Laboratory* (Woodbridge; Boydell Press, 2001), pp. 78–106.
10 Walter Scott, note 20 in the 1829 edition of *Rob Roy*, ed. Ian Duncan (Oxford: Oxford University Press, 1998), p. 459.
11 Dorothy Wordsworth, *Recollections of a Tour made in Scotland*, edit. Carol Kyros Walker (New Haven and London: Yale University Press, 1997), pp. 115, 118.
12 Samuel Coleridge, *Scottish Notes* in Carol Kyros Walker *Breaking Away: Coleridge in Scotland* (New Haven and London: Yale University Press, 2002), p. 152.
13 Ibid., p. 151.

14 Walter Scott, *The Lady of the Lake* (Edinburgh: Ballantyne 1810); new edition, Thomas Crawford (ed.), (Glasgow: Association for Scottish Literary Studies, 2010).
15 Samuel Coleridge to William Wordsworth in a letter of October 1810, in E. L. Griggs (ed.), *Collected Letters of Samuel Taylor Coleridge, volume III, 1807–1814* (Oxford: Oxford University Press, 1959).
16 These views, from the perspective of a playwright and poet as well as a scholar, were expressed to me in detailed conversation with Professor Brown on 2 September 2011.
17 Robert Cadell in J. G. Lockhart, *The Life of Sir Walter Scott*, Edinburgh Edition (Edinburgh: T. C. Jack and E. C. Jack, 1902), vol. 3, p. 217.
18 Ray McKenzie, *Public Sculpture of Glasgow* (Liverpool: Liverpool University Press, 2002), pp. 223–7 and 411–2.
19 Christopher Hibbert, *Queen Victoria: a Personal History* (London: Harper Collins, 2000), p. 478.
20 Walter Scott, *Rob Roy*, Introduction to the 1829 edition of *Rob Roy*, ed. Ian Duncan (Oxford: Oxford University Press, 1998), p. 459.
21 Walter Scott, *Waverley*, ed. P. D. Garside (Edinburgh: Edinburgh University Press, 2007), pp. 113–4.
22 Isaac Pocock, *Rob Roy or Auld Langsyne, an Operatic Drama in Three Acts* (London: John Miller, 1818).
23 See Barbara Bell, 'The National Drama, Joanna Baillie and the National Theatre', in Ian Brown *et al.* (eds.) *The Edinburgh History of Scottish Literature* (Edinburgh: Edinburgh University Press, 2007) vol. 2, pp. 228–35 and 'The National Drama and the Nineteenth Century', in Ian Brown (ed.), *The Edinburgh Companion to Scottish Drama* (Edinburgh: Edinburgh University Press, 2011), pp. 47–59.
24 Henry Cockburn, *Circuit Journeys* (Edinburgh: David Douglas, 1888), p. 26.
25 Karl Miller, *Cockburn's Millennium* (London: Duckworth, 1975), pp. 295–9.
26 Francis Jeffrey in Lord Cockburn, *Life of Francis Jeffrey* (Edinburgh: Adam and Charles Black, new edition, 1874), p. 264.
27 Henry Cockburn, ibid., pp. 25–6.
28 John Ruskin in Tim Hilton, *John Ruskin: the Early Years* (New Haven and London: Yale University Press, 2000), p. 186.
29 Effie Gray Ruskin, ibid., p. 187.
30 Sarah Murray, *A Companionable and Useful Guide to the Beauties of Scotland*, first published in 1799, ed. W. F. Laughlan (Hawick: Byway Books, 1982) p. 39.
31 Patrick Graham, *Sketches descriptive of picturesque scenery on the southern confines of Perthshire including The Trosachs and that district of the country in which the scene of the "Lady of the Lake" is laid. With notices of natural history*, (Edinburgh: Peter Hill, 1806).
32 Charles Roger, *A Week at Bridge of Allan comprising an account of the Airthrey Spa and a series of six excursions to the interesting scenery around this rising watering place* (Edinburgh: Lizars 1852, reprinted Heritage Press, 1980), p. 177.
33 Kristin Lach-Szyrma, *From Charlotte Square to Fingal's Cave: Reminiscences of a Journey through Scotland, 1820–1824*, edit. M. K. Mcleod (East Linton: Tuckwell Press, 2004), p. 197.
34 Theodor Fontane, *Beyond the Tweed: a tour of Scotland in 1858* (German original, *Jenseit des Tweed*, 1860; English translation, London: Libris, 1998).
35 Jules Verne, *The Underground City* (French original, *Les Indes noires*, 1877: English translation, Edinburgh: Luath Press, 2005).
36 Roger Bilcliffe, *The Glasgow Boys* (London: John Murray, 1984), p. 51.

37 Gerard Manley Hopkins, *Poems*, ed. R. Bridges (London: Humphrey Milford, 1918).
38 This chapter is based on an earlier contribution to *The Lie of the Land: Scottish Landscape and Culture*, a conference organised by the Stirling Centre for Scottish Studies, the University of Stirling, 26–30 July 2006.

Rob Roy: trade, improvement and the destruction of 'native' cultures

DAVID HEWITT

There are two versions of *Rob Roy*: there is the first edition published on 30 December 1817, and there is the version which appeared in two volumes in the Magnum, published in December 1829 and January 1830. John Gibson Lockhart tells us in his *Life of Scott* that:

> The title of this novel was suggested by Constable [Scott's publisher], and he told me years afterwards the difficulty he had to get it adopted by the author. [...] Constable said the name of the real hero would be the best possible name for the book. "Nay," answered Scott, "never let me have to write up to a name. You well know I have generally adopted a title that told nothing."[1]

When he had read the novel, Constable's partner in the publishing business, Robert Cadell, wrote:

> Rob [is] far from what every one expects from him—the general expectation is that Rob is to be the most unbending villain—thief —robber—rascal—but *good* in him for all that—in the Novel he has some of these traits, but figures far less on the stage than the title leads the reader to expect, indeed he appears scarcely in any shape till towards the end of the second volume—[2]

Cadell was right; there is not much of Rob Roy in the novel *Rob Roy*. Scott had not written up to the name.

However, in the Magnum edition of *Rob Roy* Scott did write up to the name, for he includes an introduction of 135 pages, the effect of which is to focus the novel upon Rob Roy. He does not base his account of the man upon contemporary written documents as David Stevenson does in his excellent study *The Hunt for Rob Roy*,[3] but largely upon stories he had heard.[4] These are often not factual, as David Stevenson has shown, but are recollections that seem to fuse different incidents and to embroider others. Scott, accounting for the wealth and variety of the stories, suggests that Rob Roy 'owed his fame in a great measure to his residing on the very verge of the Highlands, and playing such pranks in the beginning of the 18th century, as are usually ascribed to Robin Hood in the middle ages,—and that within forty miles of Glasgow, a great commercial city, the seat of a learned university'.[5] It is a nice sentence, which neatly transforms the stories of a man's serial lawbreaking into matters worthy of chuckling admiration. The effect of this long and engaging introduction is to transform the novel into a work about Rob Roy. This paper discusses the first *Rob Roy*, a novel which is not really about the man, but about the political and economic relationships of London and Northumberland, and Glasgow and the Trossachs.

Had Scott been left to his own devices he might have called his novel 'The Coming of Age of Francis Osbaldistone, Esq.', for this is a first-person narrative in which Frank tells the story of a single year in his life, 1715, the year in which he becomes 21, in other words the year in which he enters into manhood. He tells the story in 1763: a footnote reads 'This seems to have been written about the time of Wilkes and Liberty',[6] and John Wilkes was arrested for seditious libel in 1763. In other words Frank is assessing in his seventieth year a critical period in his life, which is exactly what a religious man ought to do.

In an article published in 1983 I argued that Frank's treatment of his own story shows that the spiritual significance of his journey is of primary importance to him, and thus to the novel.[7] At the beginning of his story Frank strives to show that in preparing his memoirs he is not motivated by vanity and egotism. He is not like the Duc de Sully, a man who dictated the events of his life to secretaries who then wrote them up as a third-person historical narrative and read them back to the Duke so that he could admire his own achievements (6–7); Frank hopes that some moral benefit might be obtained from considering 'the follies and headstrong impetuosity' (6) of his youth. He frequently criticises his earlier pride, presumption and self-conceit. He recognises that that part of his opposition to his father arose from a priggish distaste for generating the prosperity whose benefits he enjoyed:

> I only saw in my father's proposal for my engaging in business, a desire that I should add to those heaps of wealth which he had

himself acquired; and imagining myself the best judge of the path
to my own happiness, I did not conceive that I should increase it by
augmenting a fortune which I believed was already sufficient, and
more than sufficient, for every use, comfort, and elegant enjoyment.
(11)

He comments on his 'constitutional obstinacy' (23) and tells his friend
Tresham for whom his is writing his memoir that 'my principal fault was
an unconquerable pitch of pride' (98). This outlook was not something
recently acquired: his own story implies that adversity in 1715 was teaching
him about his own failings. When he hears of the possible ruin of his father
he exclaims to Diana:

> "[...] All this I might have prevented by a trifling sacrifice of the
> foolish pride and indolence which recoiled from sharing the labours
> of his honest and useful profession. Good Heaven! how shall I
> redeem the consequence of my error!" (142–43)

His contemplation of the tombs in the churchyard of Glasgow Cathedral
helps to put his recognition of his moral obligations into a wider religious
context:

> The contents of these sad records of mortality, the vain sorrows
> which they record, the stern lesson which they teach of the nothing-
> ness of humanity, the extent of ground which they so closely cover,
> and their uniform and melancholy tenor, reminded me of the roll of
> the prophet, which was "written within and without, and there were
> written therein lamentations and mourning and woe." (157)

The words he quotes come from Ezekiel and are apposite for they are the
summation of the message that God requires Ezekiel to deliver to the children
of Israel whom he describes as a 'rebellious nation that hath rebelled against
me: they and their fathers have transgressed against me, even unto this very
day. For they are impudent children and stiffhearted'.[8] The words that came
into Frank's head in the church yard in Glasgow suggest an unconscious
realisation that rebellion against his natural father is also rebellion against
God, and that he ought to seek reconciliation with both.

This analysis of the narratorial stance is true to what Frank says of himself, but I do not now find it convincing. He still seems to feel distaste for mercantile wealth; the dunghill image used of his father's riches, 'heaps of wealth', although nominally referring to how he felt in 1715, was written in 1763. As he writes he seems to be filled with a deep-seated melancholy that articulates itself in his religious discourse, but the words do not seem to diagnose what is wrong with him. One must observe in 1763 his beloved wife is dead, and that he is apparently childless, but he does not dwell on the one and never mentions the second. Phrases like 'unconquerable pitch of pride' which he uses of himself seem to be a stance that he takes up, not something that reveals him. There has been criticism of this aspect of the novel, from A. O. J. Cockshut and Edgar Johnson for example,[9] because the act of writing does not seem to be either cathartic or therapeutic, nor does it lead Frank to know himself better (it was his experience of 1715 which led to his enlightenment). But this is not a fault of the novel. What *is* wrong is the analysis: it expects psychological realism in the hero, but, as is true of many of Scott's heroes, he is only a means by which we look at the condition of Britain. Even although he is a participant he is best thought of as a naïve onlooker whose gifts as a writer allow him to recreate the events of 1715. We the readers are not particularly engaged with Frank the hero of the story, nor with Frank the teller of the story, but we are very engaged with what he recounts.

When my edition of *Rob Roy* appeared in 2008 I said that 'This is Scott's Hanoverian novel' (400); the declaration was meant to be provocative for *Rob Roy* is normally described as a Jacobite novel, one of the series which (in temporal order of the action in each) begins with *The Tale of Old Mortality*, goes on to *The Black Dwarf*, *Rob Roy*, *Waverley*, 'The Highland Widow', and *Redgauntlet*, a series which deals with the religious and dynastic struggle for Britain from 1679 to 1765. But it was not a rash declaration: *Rob Roy* celebrates the triumph of a new entrepreneurial spirit. There is little about war: the outbreak of the rising in September 1715 is announced by Andrew Fairservice; Frank joined General Carpenter's army which put down the rising in England, and two of Sir Hildebrand's sons fought with the Jacobites at Preston. This is the sum of the treatment of the military events of 1715, and in this respect *Rob Roy* is quite unlike *Waverley*. On the other hand, the social and the economic forces are given much more extended treatment.

Frank tells us that when they returned to London from Glasgow 'we immediately associated with those bankers and eminent merchants who agreed to support the credit of government, and to meet that run upon the Funds, on which the conspirators had greatly founded their hope of furthering their undertaking, by rendering the government, as it were, bankrupt' (317). The trigger for the rising was Rashleigh's financial plot which specifically aimed to force Highland chiefs who had raised money by selling lands and timber to William Osbaldistone, and who had been paid by promissory notes, into rebellion by making them bankrupt. The strategy was to create a credit crisis which would bring down the British government.

Rashleigh's plot fails because he underestimates both the strength and the resolve of the state. The ability of the English and from 1707 the British government to fight wars was based on its ability to finance them. The rapid development of an efficient national finance system, and the growth of the City of London as the centre for financial services, meant that the government could successfully borrow what it needed, both from major English investors and abroad in Amsterdam. Further, the large Whig majority in the Parliamentary election of January to March 1715, and the ideological compatibility of the government and City, helped to raise enough money to ensure stability. So in the year ending in Michaelmas 1716 (29 September), short-term government borrowing increased by about £1,200,000 (about 12.5%) at a rate of interest of between 5% and 5.5%, presumably to finance army expenditure which increased from £924,000 in the year ending in 1715 to £2,151,000 in 1716. This money was probably raised by subscription (i.e. by inviting known investors to lend), for the 'open' loan of 1715 failed, probably because of the jitters generated by the Jacobite rising.

In William Osbaldistone Scott combines several of the features of the government creditor: he is one of the 'bankers and eminent merchants' who subscribe to loans, and who purchase stock when it comes cheaply on to the market at times of crisis (a 'run upon the Funds': 317); he is able to raise credit through his international connections ('with funds enlarged, and credit fortified, by eminent success in his continental speculations': 312–13); he is knowledgeable about financial instruments, and hugely confident.

Baillie Nicol Jarvie is the comic parallel to William Osbaldistone: he is not a large-scale player in the way that Osbaldistone is, but it is he who articulates most memorably the moral thrust of capitalism:

"[...] But I maun hear naething about honour—we ken naething here but about credit. Honour is a homicide and a bloodspiller, that gangs about making frays in the street, but Credit is a decent, honest man, that sits at hame and makes the pat play." (206)

The recall of Falstaff may not flatter the Baillie, but it reinforces what he says, for Falstaff pronounces on the dead Sir Walter Blunt 'I like not such grinning honour as Sir Walter hath. Give me life'.[10] To the Baillie 'life' involves the making and earning of money: the proverb 'to make the pot boil' is glossed in the *Oxford Dictionary of English Proverbs* as 'to provide one's livelihood'. Jarvie (he principally) expounds self-interested benevolence in an exuberant and winning rhetoric, and it is impossible not to admire the ambition and the confidence of Osbaldistone (in spite of his ruthlessness) and Jarvie (in spite of his self-conceit). They are both practical businessmen, and within the novel they also articulate an ideology of economic development. The notes in the Edinburgh edition show that they appear to quote eighteenth-century works on business and economics such as Bernard de Mandeville's *The Fable of the Bees*, Adam Smith's *The Wealth of Nations*, Malachy Postlethwayt's *Universal Dictionary of Trade and Commerce*, Daniel Defoe's *A Tour Through the Whole Island of Great Britain*, and Thomas Pennant's *A Tour in Scotland and Voyage to the Hebrides MDCCLXXII*. Of course they are not meant to be quoting these works, every one of which was published after 1715, but giving them words from such works makes them the articulators not just of the literature but the eighteenth-century ideology of improvement via business and commerce.

And yet, Jarvie's enthusiasm begets some doubts. The analysis of Highland demographics, and the lack of work and economic opportunity, is a brilliant piece of economic modelling:

"These Hielands of ours, as we ca' them, gentlemen, are but a wild kind of warld by themsells, full of heights and hows, woods, caverns, lochs, rivers, and mountains, that it wad tire the very deevil's wings to flee to the tap o' them. [...]" (209)

Jarvie, briefly and vividly, characterises the terrain and the impossibility of making much of it productive. He goes on to calculate that the population of each parish in the Highlands and Islands was about one thousand, and, with two hundred and thirty parishes, that the total population would be around two hundred and thirty thousand. He continues:

"[...] Now, sir, it's a sad and awfu' truth, that there is neither wark, nor the very fashion or appearance of wark, for the tae half of thae puir creatures; that is to say, that the agriculture, the pasturage, the fisheries, and every species of honest industry about the country, canna employ the one moiety of the population, let them work as lazily as they like, and they *do* work as a pleugh or a spade burned their fingers. Aweel, sir, this moiety of unemployed bodies, amounting to"——

"To one hundred and fifteen thousand souls," said Owen, "being the half of the above product."

"Ye hae't, Maister Owen—ye hae't—[in each parochine] ye hae five hundred souls, the tae half o' the population, employed and maintained in a sort o' fashion, wi' some chance of sour-milk and croudie—but I wad be glad to ken what the other five hunder are to do?"

"In the name of God!" said I, "what do they do, Mr Jarvie? It makes one shudder to think of their situation."

"Sir," replied the Baillie, "ye wad may be shudder mair if ye war living near-hand them. For, admitting that the tae half o' them may make some little thing for themsells honestly in the Lowlands by shearing in harst, droving, haymaking, and the like, ye hae still mony hundreds and thousands o' lang-legged Hieland gillies that will neither wark nor want, and maun gang thigging and sorning about on their acquaintance, or live by the doing the laird's bidding, be't right or be't wrang. And mair especially, mony hundreds o' them come doun to the borders of the low country, where there's gear to grip, and live by stealing, reiving, lifting cows, and the like depredations! [...] And the lairds are as bad as the loons, for if they dinna bid them gae reive and harry, the deil a bit they forbid them, and they shelter them, or let them shelter themsells, in their woods, and mountains, and strong-holds, whenever the thing's dune. And every ane o' them will mainteen as mony o' his ain name, or his clan, as we say, as he can rap and rend means for, or, whilk's the same thing, as mony as can in ony fashion, fair or foul, mainteen themsells—and

there they are wi' gun and pistol, dirk and dourlach, ready to disturb
the peace o' the kintra whenever the laird likes—and that's the
grievance of the Hielands, whilk are, and hae been for this thousand
years bye past, a bike o' the maist lawless unchristian limmers that
ever disturbed a douce, quiet, Godfearing neighbourhood, like this
o' ours in the west here." (209–10)

Jarvie has written off half the population of the Highlands as lazy, under-
employed, dishonest, disorderly and violent. It is genocide, not in fact but
in attitude; it is the kind of nation-killing to which Sir Thomas Browne
objects in *Religio Medici*. It may seem extreme to draw this conclusion
from the words of a wonderfully comic character who provides a superbly
comic version of 'An Inquiry into the Causes which facilitate the Rise and
Progress of Rebellions and Insurrections in the Highlands of Scotland,
&c', which was a 1747 analysis of the causes of the '45, possibly written by
Robert Graham of Gartmore. But Frank objects, asking "'is it possible [...]
that this can be a just picture of so large a portion of the island of Great
Britain'" (209). And the Baillie's argument is so theoretical, so extreme, so
committed to a general conclusion and so unadmitting of any variation or
complexity, that any thinking person will not take his conclusions seriously.
He describes a model which our general experience of human nature must
lead us to reject. That it should not be accepted is borne out by the impossibility of his other great scheme, for draining Loch Lomond:

The Baillie had also his speculations, but they were of somewhat a
different complexion, as I found when, after about an hour's silence,
during which he had been mentally engaged in the calculations
necessary, he undertook to prove the possibility of draining the
lake, and "giving to plough and harrow many hundred, ay, many a
thousand of acres, from whilk no man could get earthly gude e'enow,
unless it were a gedd or a dish of perch now and then."

Amidst a long discussion, which he "crammed into mine ear
against the stomach of my sense," I only remember, that it was part
of his project to preserve a portion of the lake just deep enough
and broad enough for the purposes of water-carriage, so that coal
barges and gabbards should pass as easily between Dumbarton and
Glenfalloch as between Glasgow and Greenock. (310–11)

The idea of draining Loch Lomond (derived from Pennant) is both destructively utilitarian, and absurd. Indeed, the scheme is so daftly over-the-top that it raises scepticism about the whole of the Baillie's projecting mentality.

Our unmediated response just raises doubts, but what we are told by Diana Vernon and Rob Roy shows that the mercantile expansionism of the business community had real costs and created real pain. Diana Vernon complains:

> "[...] I belong to an oppressed sect and antiquated religion, and, instead of getting credit for my devotion, as is due to all good girls beside, my kind friend, Justice Inglewood, may send me to the house of correction, merely for worshipping God in the way of my ancestors, and say, as old Pembroke did to the Abbess of Wilton, when he usurped her convent and establishment, 'Go spin, you jade,—go spin.'" (79)

Jobson threatens Die with a series of oppressive measures—

> "Very well, ma'am—good evening, ma'am—I have no more to say —only there are laws against papists, which it would be well for the land were they better executed. There's third and fourth Edward VI., of antiphoners, missalls, grailes, processionals, manuals, legends, pies, portuasses, and those that have such trinkets in their posses-sion, Miss Vernon—and there's summoning of papists to take the oaths—and there are popish recusant convicts under the first of his present Majesty—Aye, and there are penalties for hearing mass. See twentythird Queen Elizabeth, and third James First, chapter twenty-fifth.—And there are estates to be registered, and deeds and wills to be enrolled, and double taxes to be made, according to the acts in that case made and provided"— (77)

The penal laws were haphazard and incoherent, passed at sundry times between Elizabeth's accession in 1557 and George I's death in 1727, and they stayed in force until the Catholic Relief Act of 1778, the second Catholic Relief Act of 1791, and the Catholic Emancipation Act of 1829. Broadly speaking they were intended to prevent Catholics from practising their religion, and those who did not attend the Church of England were subjected to various penalties. But for present purposes those affecting landed property are the most important. According to Richard Burn who wrote a compendium of the laws Justices of the Peace had to administer and who is extensively quoted in *Rob Roy*, 'By the yearly land tax acts, papists and reputed papists, being of 18 years of age, who shall not have taken the oaths of allegiance and supremacy, shall pay double land tax'. Northern Catholics like Sir Hildebrand had been impoverished by state oppression, and in the view of Bruce Lenman it was economic desperation which led to their involvement in the rising of 1715.[11]

The circumstances affecting Rob Roy were not the same. The MacGregors had been proscribed as a clan, but he himself was a respectable cattle dealer and landowner until he became bankrupt in 1712. In those days people unable to pay their debts were proclaimed outlaws, and so on 25 September 1712 letters of caption were issued authorising Rob Roy's capture and imprisonment until such time as he had satisfied his creditors. He owed money to the Duke of Montrose and for reasons that are not clear Montrose took the lead in trying to capture him. From this period Rob Roy considered himself to be a man unjustifiably persecuted by the Duke, and the legal processes by which debtors were criminalised turned Rob Roy into one of the Highland thieves whom Jarvie denounces. In the circumstances it is no wonder that Rob Roy protests against being 'hunted like an otter, or a sealgh, or a salmon upon the shallows, and that by my very friends and neighbours' (300). Three pages later he makes a more general protest about the treatment of the Highlanders:

"You must think hardly of us, Mr Osbaldistone, and it is not natural that it should be otherwise. But remember, at least, we have not been unprovoked—we are a rude and an ignorant, and it may be a violent and passionate, but we are not a cruel people—the land might be at peace and in law for us, did they allow us to enjoy the blessings of peaceful law—But we have been a persecuted people."

"And persecution," said the Baillie, "maketh wise men mad."

"What must it do then to men like us, living as our fathers did a thousand years since, and possessing scarce more lights than they did?—can we view their bluidy edicts against us—their hanging, heading, hounding, and hunting down an ancient and honourable name, as deserving better treatment than that which enemies give to enemies? Here I stand, have been in twenty frays, and never hurt man but when I was in het bluid, and yet they wad betray me and hang me up like a masterless dog, at the gate of ony great man that has an ill will at me." (303)

In *Rob Roy* the Osbaldistones of Northumberland and the MacGregors of the Trossachs are victims of state oppression. They live at the margins, but they have also been forcibly marginalised, turned into victims by the laws which enforce the rule and mercantile ideology of the Hanoverian state. There is something magnificent in the energy of the risk taking of William Osbaldistone and Nicol Jarvie, but it is also costly. This is also an issue in Scott's earlier Trossachs work, *The Lady of the Lake* (1810), where Roderick Dhu, the antihero, states:

> The King's vindictive pride
> Boasts to have tamed the Border-side,
> Where chiefs, with hound and hawk who came
> To share their monarch's silvan game,
> Themselves in bloody toils were snared; [...]
> The dales, where martial clans did ride,
> Are now one sheep-walk, waste and wide.
> This tyrant of the Scottish throne,
> So faithless and so ruthless known,
> Now hither comes; his end the same,
> The same pretext of silvan game.
> What grace for Highland Chiefs, judge ye
> By fate of Border chivalry.[12]

Rhoderick Dhu opposes the centralising ambitions of the Scottish monarchy in the sixteenth century, and observes that James V created a desert in the Borders and called it peace. However, this issue is not explored in the poem; it is a donnée which explains armed conflict, and it is personalised in Roderick and the King. But in the novel it is a theme whose political, sociological and economic aspects are subjected to thorough investigation. In *Rob Roy* the political and economic forces which pressurise the marginalised in Northumberland and the Highlands are exercised through laws and the legal system.

From this simple analysis I wish to draw five conclusions. In *Rob Roy* Scott examines both the phenomenon and the methods by which the state was extending its powers. Secondly, we do not, and need not, account for Frank by examining his personal psychology. He is an observer, a partici- pating observer, but also a poet who can record the passage of time, and who in telling the tale re-enacts in 1763 the events of 1715; it is not an accident that in 1715 he repeatedly thought that he had lost Die 'forever', and that in 1763 has certainly done so. Thirdly, I suggest that Frank's melan- cholia is directly associated with his perception of the cultural costs of the expansion of trade (nowadays we would call it globalisation). He married Die Vernon and in so doing he symbolically united traditions; but he has lost her; similarly the old-fashioned ways of the people of Northumberland and the Trossachs have been destroyed by modernity.

That is the kind of conclusion we can expect from any discussion of Scott, but it leads me to my fourth point, which may be more surprising. In 1715 the Hanoverian government was consolidating the modern British state; Frank Osbaldistone is writing his memoirs just as the British state was consolidating its imperial role for the novel was nominally written in 1763 at the time of Wilkes and liberty. Britain had just won the Seven Years' War; it had initially set out to defeat France but the defeat of France created the empire in the treaty of Paris in 1763. The terms of the treaty were opposed by John Wilkes, writing in the forty-fifth issue of *The North Briton* on 23 April 1763, because they let France off too lightly. In the next issue Wilkes begins by declaring: 'All of us who are Revolutioners are fully convinced that men were not made to be treated as if they were the property of any indi- vidual, who partakes of the same nature with themselves'. And he proceeds to attack Highland Chiefs whose 'vassals and tenants have always groaned under the effects of their despotic principles; the world have been witnesses, again and again, of their enslaving dispositions'.[13] The only way to reconcile Wilkes's imperialistic ambitions with his libertarian principles is to draw the conclusion that the black slave population, so greatly increased through victory over France and Spain, and Highland chiefs did not partake of the same human nature as John Wilkes. Thus *Rob Roy* is not just a Hanoverian novel. It is also an imperial novel. It is a novel which tangentially raises questions about the morality of imperial rule, and about the inevitable oppression of indigenous peoples in the interests of trade, and in the name of freedom.

Finally, *Rob Roy* also raises questions about slavery, not just by implication, but directly. It is implied that the peoples of Northumberland and the Highlands are sub-human: Diana refers to the 'Ouran-Outangs, my cousins' (81); Dugald is like one as he is 'a wild shock-headed looking animal, whose profusion of red hair covered and obscured his features' (173); and Rob Roy's width of shoulder and length of arms makes him seem like an ape (187). The Baillie possesses a West Indian estate (205). Helen MacGregor says of her husband that '"he never exchanges the tartan for the braid cloth, but he runs himself into the miserable intrigues of the Lowlands, and becomes again, after all he has suffered, their agent—their tool—their slave"' (269).

Frank Osbaldistone, writing in 1763, is deeply melancholic, and is exacerbating his misery by going over the train of events by which he won his beloved wife. He is also a cultural historian shocked at the destruction of 'native' cultures, a destruction in which he as owner of Osbaldistone Hall has participated.

Notes

1 J. G. Lockhart, *Memoirs of the Life of Sir Walter Scott, Bart.*, 7 vols (Edinburgh: Robert Cadell, 1837–38), vol. 4, p. 68.

2 National Library of Scotland, MS 322, f. 252r–v.

3 David Stevenson, *The Hunt for Rob Roy: the Man and the Myths* (Edinburgh: John Donald, 2004).

4 Walter Scott, *The Waverley Novels*, 48 vols (Edinburgh: Robert Cadell, 1829–33), vol. 7, pp. xlvi–lix.

5 Scott, *The Waverley Novels*, vol. 7, p. viii.

6 Walter Scott, *Rob Roy*, ed. David Hewitt, Edinburgh Edition of the Waverley Novels vol. 5 (Edinburgh: Edinburgh University Press, 2008), p. 32. References for subsequent quotations are given in the text.

7 David Hewitt, '*Rob Roy* and First Person Narratives', in *Scott and His Influence*, ed. J. H. Alexander and David Hewitt (Aberdeen: Association for Scottish Literary Studies, 1983), pp. 372–81.

8 Ezekiel 2. 10, 3–4.

9 A. O. J. Cockshut, *The Achievement of Walter Scott* (London: Collins, 1969), p. 164; Edgar Johnson, *Sir Walter Scott: the Great Unknown*, 2 vols. (London: Hamilton, 1970), vol. 1, p. 604.

10 *Henry IV, Part I*, 5.3.59-60; see also 5.1.124-40.

11 Richard Burn, *The Justice of the Peace and Parish Officer*, 13th edn, 4 vols (London, 1776), vol. 4, p. 13; Bruce Lenman, *The Jacobite Risings in Britain 1689–1746* (London: Methuen, 1980), p. 118.

12 Walter Scott, *The Lady of the Lake*, in *The Poetical Works of Sir Walter Scott, Bart.*, 12 vols (Edinburgh: Robert Cadell, 1833–34), vol. 8, pp. 98–99 (Canto 2, stanza 28).

13 [John Wilkes], *The North Briton*, No. 46 (Saturday, May 28, 1763), pp. 1–2.

'Woe to him who has lost his voice': re-discovering the Gaelic literature of the Lennox and Menteith

MICHAEL NEWTON

Sir Walter Scott did not discover the Trossachs, just as neither Christopher Columbus, Leif Erikson, nor Sir Henry Sinclair discovered America. Nor did he initiate literary activity in the region. There were real people living here for several thousand years engaged in their own literature before Scott penned his verses. His footnotes freely acknowledge borrowing certain narratives and motifs from the native traditions of the area in *The Lady of the Lake*, but at the same time the main body of the text itself asserts that it is giving voice to an area that has become silent. To take three short excerpts from the first Canto:

> Harp of the North! that mouldering long hast hung
> On the witch-elm that shades Saint Fillan's spring [...]

> O minstrel Harp, still must thine accents sleep?
> Mid rustling leaves and fountains murmuring [...]

> Not thus, in ancient days of Caledon
> Was thy voice mute amid the festal crowd [...]

It could be argued that James Macpherson's *Ossian* had established a trend of appropriating selected elements of Gaelic tradition and adapting them to the expectations of a contemporary anglophone audience. The problem with this trend, especially as it was extended by others such as Scott and Wordsworth, is that it enabled Gaelic literature to be eclipsed to the point that the authority of the native tradition to speak on behalf of Gaels, indeed its very existence, was undermined. This is not due to any inherent deficiency in Gaelic literature itself but is symptomatic of increasingly asymmetric power relations between Gaeldom and the anglophone world.

To be in control of one's own narrative embodies self-determination and self-realisation. The contrary condition – that of having no voice – represents a lack of power. The Gaelic language has only become moribund in the Lennox and Menteith since the 1950s or later, and yet there is surprisingly little consciousness of it today. It will seem to most visitors, indeed, most Scots, to be far south of the Highlands proper. It is clear from the literary record, however, that it was a full participant in Gaelic culture, literature, and consciousness. Indeed many literary developments are visible here before or simultaneous to their appearance elsewhere in Gaeldom. For a community to lack a voice, however, suggests that it cannot represent itself, speak its own truths, or process its own issues (to use modern jargon) using the medium most powerful and meaningful to the human condition. These ideas are reflected in a Classical Gaelic poem preserved in the early 16th-century manuscript *The Book of the Dean of Lismore*. This poem is there attributed to Donnchadh Mór ó Leamhnacht, Great Duncan of the Lennox, which Dr Steve Boardman has suggested to me could be the eighth earl of the Lennox, who was beheaded in 1425. The first quatrain states:[1]

> Mairg duine do chaill a ghuth
> Agus 'gá bhfuil sruth do dhán
> Agus nach fhéad gabháil leó
> Agus nach eól bheith 'na thámh.

> *Woe to him who has lost his voice*
> *Who has a stream of song*
> *And who cannot sing it*
> *And does not know how to be silent.*

The next two quatrains continue to depict the incompetence and impotence of the subject in aural terms, symbolised by the performance of high-register song-poetry (*dán*) and the playing of the Gaelic harp, which many Highland gentry were able to do.

When the Irish poet Muireadhach Ó Dálaigh established himself as the official poet of the Earl of the Lennox around the year 1200, he brought with him to Scotland the highly elaborate and standardised craft of Gaelic syllabic poetry, which his family had probably been pivotal in formulating.[2]

He founded what is as far as I know the longest lasting poetic dynasty in European history. It is only in the early 1700s that the MacMhuirich poets came to an end as a professional class of literati, although aspects of their legacy continued in vernacular Gaelic tradition into the twentieth century. Two poems by Muireadhach relating to Lennox patronage survive.[3] One of these, composed to Alún the Earl of Lennox, provides a kind of poetic charter for the Earl which describes him in the archetypal Gaelic fashion as a noble partner for the landscape. Muireadhach constructs a historical narrative purporting to explain the name of the river which connects it to a daughter of a king of Scotland. This poem was composed in a well established genre of Gaelic literature called *Dindsenchus* which accounts for the meaning and origin of place names. In the process, the poet demonstrates his erudition and creativity. In this case, Muireadhach established ancestral and historical credentials for the Earl in verse, probably because his family was, in reality, lacking in precisely the native roots prescribed by Gaelic ideals for leadership. The poem composed by Muireadhach to Amhlaoibh of Ardencaple, the grandson of the Earl, conveys the duties and privileges of poets in Gaelic society, possibly to stress the mutual responsibilities of the new literary dispensation. Interspersed with compliments to Amhlaoibh are demands that he pay the poet his proper wages. Towards the end of his work, Muireadhach reminds Amhlaoibh to recount and remember his ancestors, naming several of the lineages himself. Amhlaoibh can buy himself immortal fame in verse, rather than infamy, just as Muireadhach has done for his forebears in this poem itself.

Moving forward a little more than three centuries, we find a poem composed for a MacFarlane chieftain, probably Duncan who died in 1547. We can read a strong self-confidence in the powers of the professional poetic class from the content of the text itself and an assertion of the symbiotic relationship between patron and poet. For example, in the third stanza:[4]

> Théid d' eineach 's do nàire
> Thar fineachd 's ùine;
> Gach filidh ag ràdh siud:
> Gun sirear 's nach diùltar.

> *Your renown and manners*
> *Surpass kinship and time;*

Every professional poet says this:
That what is sought is found.

What is sought is, of course, payment and an adequate subject of praise. As is common in Gaelic oral tradition, the poet concludes his piece by complimenting Duncan's wife and by affirming the veracity of his words, saying *Thog mi caithream na firinn* 'I made a declaration of the truth'. After all, what would a poet's endorsement be worth if he could be bought or could not be trusted? For this reason, parenthetical remarks about honesty and accuracy are common in Gaelic texts. And so we see in this and similar poems glimpses of a robust and mature poetic tradition such as we see in other regions of Gaeldom. The major prose and poetic genres are attested here – syllabic poetry (*dán*), lyric poetry (*amhran*), strophic clan panegyric (*iorram*), piobrach song (*òran-pìobaireachd*), mouth-music (*port-á-beul*) – and variants of all of the characteristic themes and cycles have been recorded in the area, from the Ulster Cycle and the Ossianic Cycle to Jacobite themes through to life at the sheiling, all composed by Gaels for Gaels, with no sign of deficiency or anomaly. In the decade since I finished my initial attempt to gather the literary relics of the region I have found, or have been given, further examples which demonstrate the longevity and resilience of Gaelic oral tradition in the area to the end of the nineteenth century.

One of the most famous sons of the Trossachs is Rob Roy, the subject of much Gaelic and anglophone literature, each with differing perspectives. One of the items in the Gaelic repertoire is the 1735 *marbhrann* ('elegy') to Rob Roy. Ronald Black has recently edited a variant of this,[5] but I have since found a rare source which names the poet as Domhnall Breac MacGriogair, one of Rob Roy's retinue.[6] I was also given an independent variant transcribed from poet Iain MacGriogair in 1816.[7] I would like to quote the concluding three quatrains from this unique variant.

Ach mur tigeadh am Bàs
Cho aithghearr 'ad dhàil
Fhuair onoir a b' àirde fhathast uaidh.

Ach an dùthchas gu léir
Chan fheud sinn a leum
Thaobh sin, chan eil feum dhuinn labhairt orr'.

Ach bhith 'g earbsa gur feàrr [fiu?]
Comhnaidh sìorraidh nach mùth
A' toirt molaidh is cliù d'ar Tighearna.

But if Death had not come
So quickly to meet you
You [would] have yet greater honour [?].

But that entire inheritance [i.e., death]
We cannot overcome
And therefore, there's no use to speak of it.

But to trust that better
Is the eternal, unchanging state
Praising and honouring our Lord.

The purpose of elegy is to preserve in communal memory an idealised portrait of the deceased. Given that the last two stanzas are not in other surviving variants, they may be later oral accretions reflecting the increased religiosity of the late eighteenth century. Regardless of their origin, the poet attributes his duties – praising and advancing the reputation of his patron – to all people in the afterlife as they praise God, giving a particularly Gaelic flavour to the representation of heaven.

As in other spheres of literary and intellectual endeavour, Gaels in the Lennox and Menteith were often in the vanguard of religious translation and publication, as is clear from recent research by Donald Meek. Rev. Robert Kirk of Aberfoyle transliterated the Classical Gaelic translation of the Bible into Roman script and the resulting text was published in 1690, but it was in the high-register pan-Gaelic form of the language rather than vernacular Scottish Gaelic. The translation of Puritan works into Gaelic begins with the Rev. Alexander MacFarlane's *Call to the Converted* in 1750.[8] In 1753 his translations of the Psalms of David were published. In 1755 the Scottish Society for the Propagation of Christian Knowledge was arranging to translate the Bible into vernacular Scottish Gaelic and asked the Rev. Alexander MacFarlane to do the job; he could not, but Rev. James Stuart, a native of Glenfinglas who became minister of Killin, translated the New Testament, and his son, Rev. John Stuart, who became minister of Luss, revised it.⁹ Men of the cloth did not restrict themselves to godly verses. A love song considered polished and appealing enough to be included in the popular poetry anthology *Sàr Obair nam Bàrd Gaëlach*, published by John MacKenzie in 1841, was composed by Rev. Duncan Macfarlane (1771-1857).¹⁰ I will return to his father, Rev. Duncan the elder (installed as minister in Drymen parish in 1743), anon. Duncan the younger was born and raised in Drymen and took over as minister after his father died in 1791. A number of the Gaelic sermons by father and/or son to the Drymen congregation are in the Glasgow University Archives and remain unpublished. As his love song is easily obtained I will only note that even in the nineteenth century, poets from this southern tip of the Gàidhealtachd made notable contributions to the Gaelic song repertoire.

One of the interesting and unusual sources from which I drew material is a notebook of Gaelic poems, now in the National Library of Scotland. From the contents, it is clear that the author was a native of Loch Venachar named Alasdair who spent a miserable year in Glasgow. The intertwining themes of romantic love and love of homeland are dominant in nineteenth-century Gaelic poetry and in much of this manuscript. I only managed to decipher and tentatively reconstruct three poems from this source well enough to print previously. I would like to offer verses from another poem, entitled 'Litir Gaoil' ('A Love Letter'):¹¹

A nighean donn nam mala caol
Nam faodainn bhithinn cuide riut
A nighean donn nam mala caol
Nam faodainn bhithin cuide riut.

Tha mise an Glaschu nan stìopal
Àit' as coma leam dà-rìreadh
Ach is tusa, ghaoil, bhith dhìth orm
A dh'fhàg m' inntinn-sa brònach. [...]

'Sann a-raoir a bha mi 'bruadar
A bhith maille riut an uaigneas
Ann an lagan laghach luachrach
Toirt air uairean pòg dhut.

Ach 's a' mhadainn aig tràth gluasaid
An àite bhith 'g éirigh ás an luachair
Thòisich na cluig mhór' air bualadh
'S thug iad uam mo shòlas.

Ach nam faighinn-sa mo dhùrachd
Dh'fhàgainn baile mór nan luinnseach
Is b'e mo cheum a bhith sunndach
Dol do dhùthaich m' òige.

Tha mi an dòchas, ged as fheudar
Dhuinn an-dràsta bhith bho chéile,
Gum bi thusa 's mise 'na dhéidh seo
Luidh is ag éirigh còmhla.

Ach, a ghaoil, na leig air dìochuimhne
Alasdair, ged tha e dhìth ort
Is creid gum bi e daingeann dìleas
Is fìrinneach ri bheò dhut.

O brunette girl of the slender brows
I'd be with you if I could
O brunette girl of the slender brows
I'd be with you if I could.

I am in Glasgow of the steeples,
A place about which I truly do not care
But it is your absence, darling,
Which has left my mind dejected. [...]

Last night I was dreaming
That I was alone with you
In a pleasant hollow full of rushes
Giving you occasional kisses.

But in the morning, at waking time,
Rather than emerging from the rushes

The great bells began to ring
And they took my solace from me.

But if I could get my wish
I would leave the big city of the watch-coats
My step would be merry
Going to the land of my youth.

I am hopeful that, although we must
Currently be apart,
You and I will, after this,
Lie down and arise together.

But, darling, do not forget
Alasdair, although he is not with you,
And believe that he will be faithful
And honest to you all his life.

The poetry in this manuscript consists of highly personal and localised poetry, drawing on many common motifs, but I assess it as being of a high standard, indicating that literary tradition was still strong even amongst the youth of this time (apparently sometime in the nineteenth century). Alasdair is communicating his love to his beloved in poetic form, and the transition from oral to written transmission of that message is marked in the title of the piece itself. Indeed, the self-conscious recognition of this development is evident in other pieces from the area.[12]

Atholl poet Donnchadh Mac an Tòisich (1804–c. 1846), known by the nickname 'Am Bàrd Mùgach' ('The Gloomy Poet'), published a booklet of Gaelic poetry in 1832.[13] Although he was not a native of the area, one item in this booklet is very interesting for what it says about connections between areas within Highland Perthshire and the social rôle of the poet. The poet relates his knowledge of Ben Venue in an authoritative manner, and like the *Dindsenchus* genre of old, he uses the poetic conceit of a challenge as an excuse to offer his opinion:

Aithris dhuinne, Mhic an Tòisich,
On is fear sgeòil thu tha gabhail seachad

Eachdraidh na beinne móire
Tha chòmhnaidh aig ceann Loch Ceiteir.

Eachdraidh air a' Bheinne Mheanabh
Dhut le dearbh gun d'thoir mi seachad
A' bheinn ard chreagach chorrach gharbh
Am faigh na balgairean am fasgadh.

A' bheinn ard chorrach gharbh
A thug barrachd air beanntan na h-Alba
A' bheinn air nach fhaicear am fraoch
Ach creagan raithneach is maoilean gorm. [...]

Shiubhail mi Alba ma cuairt
Na bha eadar Tuaid is Arcaibh
Ach thug mi an t-urram [] 'n suairceas
Da'n tuath tha ma thaobh Loch Ceiteir.

Daoine còire gun ghruaim,
Mnathan òg' suairce tlachdmhor,
Maighdeinean banail stuam –
B'e mo thruaigh gun bhith an taic ribh.

Relate to us, o Macintosh,
As you are a passing storyteller,
The history of the great mountain
That sits at the end of Loch Katrine.

The history of Ben Venue
I shall truly give to you
The tall, rough, steep, craggy mountain
In which the foxes find shelter.

The tall, steep, rough mountain
That excelled Scotland's mountains
The mountain on which no heather is seen
But only bracken-covered craigs and green bare-spots. [...]

I have travelled all around Scotland
Between the Tweed and Orkney
But I give the honour in kindness
To the folk who live around Loch Katrine.

Goodly and good-natured people,
Young, kind, enjoyable women,
Feminine, modest girls –
I would be sad to be away from you.

The poem is meant as a compliment to the people of Loch Katrine-side, who must have been able to understand his message. To be sure, Gaelic was still spoken by many of what population was left into the early twentieth century. It is surely worth considering the suggestion,[14] even though insufficient information survives to evaluate it, that Donnchadh is asserting the primacy of this location in direct response to the local competing claims resulting from the imaginative and tourist-oriented literature and entrepreneurial tourism, explored in detail in the other chapters in this volume. The poet's geographical terms of reference are significant as well: for him, the integral territory was Scotland, from Tweed to Orkney. This is one of many examples of the assertion of the essential unity of Scotland in Gaelic verse, even as its identity was being reformulated in English as 'North Britain'. Donnchadh asserts that his knowledge of Scotland qualifies him to honour Loch Katrine-side with special distinction.

There are few events with as much impact on Gaelic literary history as the publication and reception of James Macpherson's *Ossian* in the 1760s, for better and worse, so before going on, a brief discussion is in order to dispel some popular misconceptions. Indeed, it is primarily due to the dispute over the authenticity of *Ossian* that fieldwork began to be carried out as to the contents and condition of Gaelic oral tradition amongst the peasantry, and by documenting these previously untapped sources a new and diverse set of voices was revealed. Macpherson's claims that he had translated Gaelic poetry directly into English were false, but neither is *Ossian* exactly the fraud or forgery which it is often claimed to be. Macpherson was a native Gaelic speaker who was actually familiar with real heroic oral poetry circulating in the Highlands and attributed traditionally to Oisean, son of Fionn mac Cumhaill. Macpherson selected certain themes, plots, and motifs from

Gaelic literature and wove them into his own text according to the expectations of his contemporary audience. Extensive research by scholars for over a century has demonstrated both his personal creativity and his debt to tradition. However, given the fulsome praise bestowed upon *Ossian* and the general disdain with which Highlanders were otherwise regarded, most contemporary Gaels were willing to overlook his fabrications and give him their seal of approval. Many natives were familiar with fragments of Ossianic poetry, but Gaelic oral tradition was already perceived as weakened and disintegrating. It did not require excessive suspension of critical thinking to believe that Macpherson had found a pure source uncontaminated by the vagaries of oral transmission.[15]

Not only was Ossianic material composed and recited in the Lennox and Menteith, as in the rest of the Gàidhealtachd, but placenames confirm the Fenian 'cult' and the likely relocalisation of Fenian lore in the region.[16] Indeed, Macpherson was still writing in 1763 when Rev. Duncan MacFarlane (the elder) confirmed that Ossianic lore was once universal but now only retained by the elderly on Loch Lomond-side.

> This part of the country is at some distance from the scene of action and the prevailing of the English language hath very near banished the Gaelick and alongst with it, the recitals of the actions of the Fians – Only some few old people retain some fragments, which they repeat [...] I do remember in my early days to have heard the exploits of the Fians recited almost by everybody [...][17]

In this account and others, the loss of this once esteemed lore is connected to the sudden social and economic ascendency of the anglophone world and, with it, the marginalisation of Gaelic language and culture. Rev. Patrick Graham, minister of Aberfoyle, recorded in 1798:

> I need not inform you, who know this neighbourhood so well, that on these outskirts of the Highlands, little attachment to ancient observances, and few remains of ancient traditions are to be expected. Our vicinity to, and frequent intercourse with the Low Country, have almost obliterated every trace of the Antiquities – and much of the language of our Forefathers – 'Tis true, every Highlander, even in this neighbourhood, who is advanced in life, has heard of Fingal

& of his heroes (*Gaisgich na Féinne*) and recollects well that it was amongst the amusements of his youth to hear the Poems that relate to them rehearsed. But there is nobody now living hereabouts, that I know of, who can himself repeat any of those ancient productions & so rapid is the progress, at present, towards the total oblivion of our ancient traditions and language, (especially on these Borders of the Highlands) that I have no difficulty in supposing that, with one Generation more, there will be little known of Ossian, and the subjects of his song, except what is derived from written record.

[...] Since writing the above, my father informs me that there is an old man still alive – a Robert McNeil at Corry in the parish of Drymen, whom he has frequently heard repeating Gaelic poems said to be Ossians. My father remembers the father of this Macniel, who was eminent in his day for his knowledge of those poems, and he particularly recollects his having heard the old man reciting a long poem, the subject of which was the invasion of Scotland by the King of Denmark (*Rìgh Lochlinn*).[18]

Thus, there were still people in the parish of Drymen who knew Ossianic verse ('Laoidh Mhànuis', in this case) in the nineteenth century. In his 1806 book, Graham confirms that MacNeil was still living and that another man, S. MacLachlane in Aberfoyle parish, knew the heroic lay 'Laoidh Fhraoich'.[19]

Some of the most vicious attacks on Macpherson's claims and the possibility that Gaels had a legitimate literary culture came from Lowland Scots Malcolm Laing and John Pinkerton.[20] Rev. John Buchanan, a native Gaelic speaker from Leny, near Callander, responded to the racist diatribes of Pinkerton with the book *A Defence of the Scots Highlanders* in 1794. In the preface he tactfully points out that Pinkerton's ignorance of Gaelic as a living language, and his complete reliance on non-Gaelic texts, makes him a poor judge of the origins and nature of the Ossianic texts.

How far the following attempt, to throw light on a subject which has hitherto been looked upon as a kind of fable, will merit the first or last of these decision, is by the Author left to stand or fall by the judgment of the impartial Public, before whom it is now to make its appearance. He only has to say for himself, that his sole aim is,

if possible, to snatch from oblivion, and bring into repute, circumstances which to him appeared to have been misunderstood and
neglected, in spite of the living language of an ancient people, that
plainly indicate their having had an existence. Yet the many able and
learned gentlemen, who from age to age have laboured to do honour
to their country, have unfortunately been strangers to the language,
and rested secure upon the authorities handed down by the old
Greeks and Romans, as to infallible standards of appeal, though
it is beyond a doubt that their own knowledge of the subject was
but extremely imperfect, and their information from second-hand
behoved to be limited, or at best but misinformed authority.[21]

Buchanan more forcefully states that the poor status of Gaelic was no
accident of history, but that, despite adversity, it had survived relatively
intact. 'Gaelic is the longest preserved to this day, and is pretty free from
mixture and corruption, notwithstanding the disadvantages it had to
struggle with, from the strong attempts made to destroy it.'[22]

The 'Age of Improvement' promised that not only material conditions,
but also cultural heritage, could be developed. Some Highlanders were
hopeful that Gaelic might reap some of these benefits. John MacFarlan,
farmer in Auchaltie, Drymen parish, wrote to the Highland Society of
Edinburgh around the beginning of the nineteenth century to encourage
the gentlemen leaders to act in concert to provide the tools and social
leverage necessary to level the playing field so that Gaelic could have a fair
chance in the modern world.

Understanding that the honourable Highland Society in Edinburgh
wish to improve the Gaelic language, I therefore recommend to
them to cause it to be learnt in all the branches of learning, that
the Highlanders will be enabled to transact business in their own
language and not compelled to learn the English tongue before they
can do any business whatever.[23]

Unfortunately, however, this precocious vision of linguistic development
in high registers and formal institutions went largely unheeded until quite
recently, and the Lennox and Menteith were some of the first areas to suffer
the ethnocidal impact of anglocentric hegemony. The loss of the Gaelic

language has been accompanied by the loss of access to both oral tradition and written literature of great age and beauty.

The literary conceit in *The Lady of the Lake* that the native minstrel harp of the Highlands generally, or of the Trossachs specifically, had fallen asleep until he aroused it is, then, clearly fraudulent. Native Gaels were still actively engaged in their own literary tradition when Scott's poem was published and long afterwards. However we may judge the literature of Scott, whether according to the standards of English literature of his times or of our own, what is galling is that it is this literature that has come to represent the Trossachs to the exclusion of that composed in Gaelic by the natives themselves over many centuries. The trenchant anti-Ossianic camp reinforced negative attitudes about Gaelic literary tradition and many refused to acknowledge that it had one. These prejudices have continued to sour perceptions in many quarters to the present. While Gaelic literature has had a very different trajectory of development from English literature, and operates according to a different set of parameters, it deserves to be recognised as legitimate in its own right and on its own terms.[24] The anglophone tradition has deeply colonised the Highland landscape and the metaphorical literary landscape, and the post-colonial project of recognising, reclaiming, and revitalising Gaelic tradition has barely begun. It is particularly through this medium that the people of this region expressed their hopes, fears, delights, and desires. Their voices have a right to be heard and their literature deserves to be rediscovered.

Acknowledgments

Thanks to the Trustees of the National Library of Scotland for permission to print from manuscripts Acc. 9134 and Adv. MS 73.2.13.

I wish to express my deepest gratitude to ASLS for making it possible for me to attend the annual ASLS conference at which I presented a paper on which this chapter is based by supporting my travel costs.

Notes

1   William J. Watson (ed.) *Bàrdachd Albannach O Leabhar Deadhan Lios-Móir / Scottish Verse from the Book of the Dean of Lismore* (Scottish Gaelic Texts 1), (Edinburgh: Scottish Gaelic Texts Society, 1937), pp. 248–9.

2   Katharine Simms, 'Muireadhach Albannach Ó Dálaigh and the Classical Revolution', in Ian Brown *et al.* (eds.) *The Edinburgh History of Scottish Literature* (Edinburgh: Edinburgh University Press, 2007) vol. 2, pp. 83–90.

3   Thomas Owen Clancy (ed.) *The Triumph Tree: Scotland's Earliest Poetry AD 550–1350* (Edinburgh: Canongate, 1998), pp. 258–62.

4   Michael Newton (ed.) *Bho Chluaidh gu Calasraid / From the Clyde to Callander* (Stornoway: Acair, 1999), pp. 166–7.

5   Ronald Black (ed.), *An Lasair: Anthology of 18th Century Scottish Gaelic Verse* (Edinburgh: Birlinn, 2001), pp. 144–9.

6   Gregor MacGregor (ed.), *Ceileairean Binn nan Creagan Aosda* (Glasgow: D. McKenzie, 1819), p. 31.

7   Michael Newton, 'Early Poetry in the MacGregor Papers', *Scottish Gaelic Studies*, 21 (2003), 47–58 (pp. 48–9). The article contained a typo about the variant's length: it is 23 (not 33) stanzas.

8   Donald Meek, 'The pulpit and the pen: clergy, orality and print in the Scottish Gaelic world', in Adam Fox and Daniel Woolf (eds.) *The Spoken Word, Oral Culture in Britain, 1500–1850* (Manchester: Manchester University Press, 2002), pp. 84–118 (p. 91).

9   Donald Mason, 'James Stuart of Killin', *Highland Monthly*, 1 (1889), pp. 494–9; Meek, 'The pulpit and the pen', p. 94.

10 Born 1708 in Pollochrow.

11 NLS Acc. 9134. There are two other verses of this poem for which I cannot yet provide definitive edition.

12 Especially *Bho Chluaidh*, pp. 264–7.

13 Michel Byrne, 'Mairearad Ghriogarach: Sùil Thòiseachail air Bana-Bhard air Dìochuimhne', *Scottish Gaelic Studies*, 23 (2007), 85–122 (p. 87).

14 Made to me by Tom Furniss during discussions at the ASLS conference, 'Scott, the Trossachs and the Tourists', Balloch, 5–6 June 2010.

15 Donald Meek, 'The Sublime Gael: The Impact of Macpherson's "Ossian" on Literary Creativity and Cultural Perception in Gaelic Scotland', in Howard Gaskill (ed.), *The Reception of Ossian in Europe* (London: Thommes, 2004), pp. 40–66.

16 *Bho Chluaidh*, pp. 54–7.

17 NLS Adv MS 73.2.13, old item #3, new folio 14.

18 NLS Adv MS 73.2.13, old item #36, folio 70.

19 Patrick Graham, *Sketches descriptive of picturesque scenery, on the southern confines of Perthshire* (Edinburgh: Peter Hill, 1806), p. 93. A gravestone in the Drymen churchyard implies that the MacLachlanes were centred around Achantroig.

20 William Fergusson, *The Identity of the Scottish Nation: An Historic Quest* (Edinburgh: Edinburgh University Press, 1998), p. 245.

21 John Buchanan, *A Defence of the Scots Highlanders* (London: Edgerton, 1794), pp. i–ii.

22 Buchanan, p. 21.

23 Ronald Black, 'The Gaelic Academy: The Cultural Commitment of the Highland Society of Scotland', *Scottish Gaelic Studies*, 14 (1986), pp. 1–38 (p. 14).

24 William Gillies, 'On the Study of Gaelic Literature', in Michel Byrne, Thomas Owen Clancy & Sheila Kidd (eds.) *Litreachas & Eachdraidh: Rannsachadh na Gàidhlig 2, Glaschu 2002 / Literature & History: Papers from the Second Conference of Scottish Gaelic Studies, Glasgow 2002* (Glasgow: University of Glasgow, 2006), pp. 1–32.

On the look-out for beauty:
Dorothy Wordsworth in the Trossachs

DOROTHY McMILLAN

William and Dorothy Wordsworth visited the Trossachs twice during their 1803 tour of Scotland.[1] My title derives from an episode during their first visit, when they were still accompanied by Coleridge. It is an episode which seems to typify the behaviour of all three. The party, having approached the Trossachs the 'wrong way' from west to east, have arranged to be rowed down Loch Katrine (Ketterine in Dorothy Wordsworth's spelling). The day was rainy and cold, with a strong wind.

> C. was afraid of the cold in the boat, so he determined to walk down the lake, pursuing the same road we had come along. There was nothing very interesting for the first three or four miles on either side of the water: to the right, uncultivated heath or poor coppice-wood, and to the left, a scattering of meadow ground, patches of corn, coppice-woods, and here and there a cottage. The wind fell, and it began to rain heavily. On this William wrapped himself in the boatman's plaid, and lay at the bottom of the boat till we came to a place where I could not help rousing him. We were rowing down that side of the lake which had hitherto been little else than a moorish ridge. After turning a rocky point we came to a bay closed in by rocks and steep woods, chiefly of full-grown birch. The lake was elsewhere ruffled, but at the entrance of this bay the breezes sunk, and it was calm: a small island was near, and the opposite shore, covered with wood, looked soft through the misty rain. William, rubbing his eyes, for he had been asleep, called out that he hoped I had not let him pass by anything that was so beautiful as this; and I was glad to tell him that it was but the beginning of a new land. (I, 271)

Coleridge seems separatist and a bit timid; Wordsworth selfish and self-absorbed – he not only protects himself but takes the boatman's plaid to do so – and Dorothy selflessly remains on the look-out for beauty to convey to her brother. But that sense that this episode sums up the travellers is an illusion and should teach us not to judge places or people too quickly: both Scotland and these travellers within it are more complicated, less easily pinned down than this passage suggests. Coleridge did leave the Wordsworths at Arrochar three days later, the plan being to send his bag to Edinburgh and return there on foot, but in the end, no namby-pamby he, he began an extravagant walking tour of his own – 263 miles in eight days, splitting his shoes, looking more and more like a madman as he proceeded in an adventure that needs, and has been given, its own narrative.[2] William, to be sure, had already been described by Samuel Rogers who met the group in Dumfries, as so absorbed in talking to Coleridge about poetry, 'that the whole care of looking out for cottages where they might [...] pass the night, as well as of seeing their poor horse fed and littered, devolved upon Miss Wordsworth';[3] and Wordsworth had also distinguished himself the day before by dropping their food bundle into Loch Katrine: it consisted of two fowls 'which were no worse' and some sugar, ground coffee, and pepper-cake which unsurprisingly seemed 'to be entirely spoiled' (1, 259). But Dorothy says that they saw Samuel Rogers and his sister for only a quarter of an hour (1, 198) and so we may assume his account was a little coloured by amused malice. William, if we believe Dorothy, and we have no other guide to this, took all the care of horse and car and 'gained most of his road-knowledge from ostlers' (1, 235), who also informed him, if not always reliably, about inns: Wordsworth was actually quite an efficient traveller.

And Dorothy herself emerges from the *Recollections* as both more and less than a mere guide for her brother. Dorothy is famous for her eye, but the special visual quality, the essential quality of the scenery of the Trossachs, or indeed any other part of Scotland that they visited, proved hard for Dorothy to convey. Indeed, the notion of Dorothy as a kind of tour-guide whose main function was to point out the sights to the tourist William, and subsequently to write about them, to fix their experiences for the future, is not one that would have appealed much to either of them. Like some before them and like many after them, the Wordsworths did not quite see themselves as tourists: tourists, as we know, are always other people.

Nor did the Wordsworths have a very high opinion of tourist literature; like their friend Stoddart before them, they tended to disparage the genre to which they were contributing. '*Tours*,' says John Stoddart in his

Preface to his *Remarks on Local Scenery and Manners in Scotland*, 'are the mushroom produce of every summer, and Scotland has had her share'.[4] When there was some possibility that Samuel Rogers would secure the publication of her *Recollections* in 1823, Dorothy wrote to him that she feared that a 'work of such slight pretensions will be wholly overlooked in this writing and publishing (especially *tour*-writing and *tour*-publishing) age'.[5] More generally deprecating her travel writing she writes on 16 January 1822 to Catherine Clarkson that compared to her brother's poetry, her own narratives are of: 'Events unimportant and lengthy descriptions [...] which can only interest friends'. Her brother's poems, on the other hand, 'are as good as a descriptive tour – without describing'.[6]

Central to her feelings about description is the sense that the authentic experience is an imaginative and poetic one. Experience of the physical world, natural and human, may, indeed must, feed the poet, but the writing of descriptive tours for their own sake is a relatively lowly activity, an act of friendship, perhaps, but not a self-authenticating act nor one which provides anything as significant as poetry. This uneasiness about the status of travel writing repeatedly gets into the *Recollections* themselves and gives them their special unsettled character, despite what often seems like a very decided, even authoritative air. Are they or are they not travel writing? I want to suggest that it is this refusal of the *Recollections* to conform to any clear generic mould that makes them unique both in travel writing and in autobiographical writing, or self-writing as it is now often called.

Most modern travel writing involves writing up a journal after a return home. It is recollective but is generally based on notes that are close to the actual experiences. The *Recollections* are singular in being composed from memory some time after the actual experiences. Dorothy insists in several letters and in annotations to the MSS of her travels that, 'I am writing not a Journal, *for we took no notes*, but *recollections* of our Tour in the form of a Journal'.[7] The first visit to the Trossachs is recorded in the part of the journal which was begun on 24 September 1803, soon after the Wordsworths returned from their trip. It was then interrupted on 20 December by the arrival in Grasmere of Coleridge paying a farewell visit before his departure for Malta. The second visit to the Trossachs from east to west, following the more conventional route, was recorded some time later, after a number of vicissitudes, including the tragic death of her brother, John, in the shipwreck of the Abergavenny in February 1805. On 11 April Dorothy writes in the

Recollections of resuming her task, 'I am setting about a task which, however free and happy the state of my mind, I could not have performed well at this distance of time; but, now, I do not know that I shall be able to go on with it at all' (1, 344).

This is her most anxious remark, but references to personal and compositional insecurities are scattered throughout the work even in its early stages: 'Perhaps you will think that there is not much in this, as I describe it' (1, 239); 'partly from laziness, and still more because it was inconvenient, I took no notes and now am little better for what he [their Highland driver in Glencoe] told me' (1, 331); 'I wish I had written down [...] some interesting facts [...] while they were fresh in my memory' (1, 355); 'I now at this distance of time regret that I did not take notes' (1, 390); 'I wish I could have given you a better idea of what we saw between Peebles and this place. I have most distinct recollections of the effect of the whole day's journey; but the objects are mostly melted together in my memory, and though I should recognise them if we revisit the place, I cannot call them out so as to represent them to you with distinctness' (1, 393).

But in spite of Dorothy's protestations the *Recollections* are travel writing of a high, if unconventional, kind. They achieve her declared aim to make her readers feel that they have been there, and that they understand how specific places affected their friends, William and Dorothy Wordsworth and briefly Coleridge too; that, in short, they have shared an experience of these places as they were at a particular moment. And because they are addressed to friends, the self that composes and the selves that are revealed are peculiarly important. These selves, these friends of the readers, can be understood through the effects of place on their imaginations. Yet, this brings another series of problems – it is not merely that the failure to take notes may damage accuracy, but that the very process of writing down may be denaturing.

A series of conventions had been gradually growing up to express the effect of the natural world on the imagination of the viewer, producing a visual code with which Dorothy Wordsworth was perfectly familiar and which she knew could act as a kind of shorthand for her readers. But Dorothy Wordsworth is anxious both to acknowledge these conventions, this visual code, and at the same time refuse to be trapped by them. An examination of the use of the period's key descriptive words in the *Recollections* is revealing: 'sublime' which one might have expected to occur with some frequency in Scotland, even as an apology for more deserted places, occurs only five times: four usages are literary, rather than directly referring to the landscape, and the fifth is in a famous passage which humorously casts doubt on all the claims of the visual code. Coleridge has been chatting with a gentleman about the waterfall Cora Linn; the gentleman remarks that it is a '*majestic* waterfall':

> Coleridge was delighted with the accuracy of the epithet, particularly as he had been settling in his own mind the precise meaning of the words grand, majestic, sublime, etc., and had discussed the subject with Wm. at some length the day before. 'Yes, sir,' says Coleridge, 'it *is* a majestic waterfall.' 'Sublime and beautiful,' replied, his friend. Poor C. could make no answer, and, not very desirous to continue the conversation, came to us and related the story, laughing heartily. (1, 224)

'Beautiful' is used too many times to remark – I stopped counting after fifty; 'pretty' is also used frequently, but less frequently simply to characterise a scene – often it rather characterises a child, a house, a garden and so on. The usages of 'picturesque' are interesting because they are so sparing. The word is used in the text itself only five times and once in Shairp's notes about the Trossachs. Dorothy remarks once that a line of coal carts crossing the tranquillity of a glen 'add much to the picturesque effect of the different views' (1, 205), once it refers to the Trongate, once to Blair Castle, once refers disparagingly to the 'traveller who goes in search of the picturesque' (1, 390). The most telling usage occurs in the Trossachs when the boatman is anxious to point out the best bits:

> he would often say, after he had compassed the turning of a point, 'This is a bonny part,' and he always chose the bonniest, with greater skill than our prospect-hunters and 'picturesque travellers;' places screened from the winds—that was the first point; the rest followed of course,—richer growing trees, rocks and banks, and curves which the eye delights in. (1, 271)

It is the boatman, the resident of these parts who has the most reliable sense of what makes the observer both comfortable, 'screened from the winds', and surprised by the prevailing order in variety, *concordia discors*. Of course, the meaning of the placename, Trossachs (which Dorothy Wordsworth incidentally gets wrong), itself invokes the picturesque principle of order in variety: 'the rough and bristly country'.

The most memorable imaginative vision in *The Recollections* occurs in the Trossachs but presents an indoor landscape, an interior in more senses than one. It occurs in the ferryhouse after the Wordsworths' return from their tour of the loch.

> I went to bed some time before the family. The door was shut between us, and they had a bright fire, which I could not see; but the light it sent up among the varnished rafters and beams, which crossed each other in almost as intricate and fantastic a manner as I have seen the under-boughs of a large beech-tree withered by the depth of the shade above, produced the most beautiful effect that can be conceived. It was like what I should suppose an under-ground cave or temple to be, with a dripping or moist roof, and the moonlight entering in upon it by some means or other, and yet the colours were more like melted gems. I lay looking up till the light of the fire faded away, and the man and his wife and child had crept into their bed at the other end of the room. I did not sleep much, but passed a comfortable night, for my bed, though hard, was warm and clean: the unusualness of my situation prevented me from sleeping. I could hear the waves beat against the shore of the lake; a little 'syke' close to the door made a much louder noise; and when I sate up in my bed I could see the lake through an open window-place at the bed's head. Add to this, it rained all night. I was less occupied by remembrance of the Trossachs, beautiful as they were, than the vision of the Highland hut, which I could not get out of my head. I thought of the Fairyland of Spenser, and what I had read in romance at other times, and then, what a feast would it be for a London pantomime-maker, could he but transplant it to Drury Lane, with all its beautiful colours! (1, 277–78)

The movement of the mind displaces the physical scenery into a mental landscape, yet also links the natural to romance literary tradition and popular entertainment: it is a democratic mode of perception, and a poetic one, and one that importantly begins and ends in sociability.

This extraordinary vision elevates the writing to a kind of poetry and invokes the vital role of memory in forming the self and giving it a history in places – it is in this way authenticating. But in another sense it is so removed from the actual places, so much an ideal vision, that it would be possible to suspect that it did not occur in the Trossachs at all. Countering this, Dorothy Wordsworth, I think probably quite artfully, interposes episodes of discomfort and even misery. A number of Scottish inns are dirty and inhospitable, the dropsical landlady at Luss is 'the most cruel and hateful woman I ever saw' (1, 250), and the food on several occasions is quite disgusting. The Wordsworths' discomforts are scrupulously recorded and work to authenticate the tour. But if this discomfort is authenticating, it is also alienating. So too is what has sometimes been felt to be a charac-teristically English disgust with Scottish dirtiness and sloth.

Dorothy Wordsworth uses the word 'dirty' very often in her *Recollections*; sometimes even in her descriptions of the Trossachs and surrounding areas. Of the interior of the Tarbet boatman's hut she writes: 'within I never saw anything so miserable from dirt, and dirt alone' (1, 259). Even if you believe in the dirt, such observations make Dorothy Wordsworth rather unattractive to some modern readers. When I taught the *Recollections* in a Romanticism Masters course a number of the students, British, American, and from the Far East remarked this: 'Why does she keep going on about places and people being dirty?' they asked. 'Perhaps because they were', I said. 'Even so,' they said.

Yet the general attitude of Dorothy Wordsworth to Scottish dirt accords only too well with Scott's Tully-Veolan. Significantly, however, praise of Scottish civility and Scottish pride in place, also feature prominently. The workers in the fields of Mr Macfarlane's farm at Glengyle are admittedly amused by the Wordsworths' aim of seeing the Trossachs: 'no doubt they thought we had better have stayed at our own homes' but the Trossachs boatman 'is attached to the lake by some sentiment of pride, as his own domain' and has a rare sense of what is fitting behaviour to the travellers in his own home: he is courteous and attentive without servility, and his sense of how memory and retelling are part of travel is joyful and sensitive, as he repeats 'from time to time that we should often tell of this night when we got to our own homes' (1, 277).

There is no sign of Peter Bellish insensibility here – and this is authen-ticating, too. No one could have made this up – the boatman with a few touches becomes as real to us as Loch Katrine is to him. And it is perhaps Dorothy Wordsworth's representation of the people she meets that is the most moving achievement of the *Recollections*. It has in our gender-conscious period been frequently remarked that Dorothy provides insight into the nature and significance of the domestic lives of the women she encounters, thus exploring a dimension of experience that passes by her male companions. But I think it is more than this: it is her desire to give *everyone* she meets a context and a history that makes her different from William, even when it is William's vision and not her own that she admires. Some of William's most famous poems had their source in the two visits to the Trossachs: 'The Highland Girl', 'Stepping Westward' and 'The Solitary Reaper'. In all three the imaginative experience depends on mysteries not being cleared up. But Dorothy Wordsworth's object is generally to remove mystery, to give more and more information until the people she meets, men and women, acquire a life independent of her own imaginings. When on the first Trossachs trip the ferryman apologises for the bad weather, the Wordsworths console themselves that their misty view is more romantic – it may be so, but the ferryman's point of view is allowed its own cred-ibility. By the time they return to the Trossachs the ferryman has become 'our old friend'—he is perfectly unmysterious and so is the landscape. 'It was no longer a visionary scene: the sun shone into every crevice of the hills, and the mountain tops were clear. After some time we went into the pass from the Trossachs, and were delighted to behold the forms of objects fully revealed, and even surpassing in loveliness and variety what we had conceived' (1, 366). That second sight of the Trossachs validates the ferry-man's original distress at bad weather – it proves not to be a disappointment to see clearly.

Indeed Dorothy's treatment of the people she meets insofar as it leads to clarification, could be characterised as letting the sunlight in, while William prefers rather to keep it out, to prefer the mystery of shade. He imagines a relationship with the Highland Girl by not enquiring too closely into what *she* would like, whereas Dorothy on her return to Scotland nineteen years later with Joanna Hutchison wonders about what has become of the Highland Girl and the other inhabitants of the hut at Inversneyde:

Poor thing! I ask myself in vain what has become of *her*? And that little Babe that squalled the harder while its Grandame rocked, as if

to stifle its cries. Brought up in toil and hardship, is it still struggling
on? Or, with the aged woman, sleeping in the quiet grave? (2, 353)

It is always real lives of men and women that Dorothy tries to imagine.

Dorothy Wordsworth's recollections travelled back to Scotland on a
number of occasions: in 1807 with her old friend Jane Pollard, now Mrs
John Marshall to whom Dorothy writes from Grasmere on 19 September
1807: 'I am sorry that our host, Macgregor, has left the Ferryhouse at Loch
Ketterine, and I do not regret as he was not there that you did not go up
the Lake'.[8] And, of course, Dorothy's account went with William and Mary
when they toured with Sara Hutchison in 1814. Sara showed an interest in
the people she encountered that was possibly stimulated by her reading of
Dorothy's recollections. In her journal Sara writes of a household in the
Trossachs: 'The man sat making a rake and conversed sensibly upon all
subjects – he had an excellent library in the *spence* – many new books such
as Mrs Grant on the Highlands, Scott's poems and many county histories –
besides some old books of value'.[9]

Dorothy Wordsworth took the Trossachs with her when she travelled
on the Continent in 1820: when she is unable to sleep at an Inn in the
Valley of Trientz, she 'thought of Loch Ketterine, and that open window at
my bed's head [...] and rose in the middle of the night to look out upon
the mountains' (2, 293). And she finds that the wooden-walled apartments,
although neater, are 'not so warm as the stone ones of our Ferryman at
Loch Ketterine' (2, 294). And, as I have indicated, she took her recollections of the Highland Girl with her on her return to Scotland in 1822 with
Joanna Hutchison, *her* friend and Mary Wordsworth's sister, although she
did not on this occasion make an extensive tour of the Trossachs.

The account of her 1803 Scottish visit was not published in her life-time.
The story of the attempts to publish is told by De Selincourt in the preface
to his 1941 edition where he describes the MSS of the work. And when I
saw for myself in the Wordsworth Trust Library at Grasmere the denaturing
changes that were made to the MS in 1822–23 with a view to publication, I
can echo wholeheartedly De Selincourt's relief that publication was aborted.
But it is her second tour that reveals, I think, the underlying reasons for
Dorothy Wordsworth's failure to publish her recollections of the 1803 tour.
Any publication after 1822 would have been coloured by her awareness
that things had changed since 1803. She could not possibly have retained

intact the notion of the self-contained travellers that she and William and Coleridge had been in 1803. The second tour was a much more public affair. And Dorothy's mode of writing had changed, too. The *Recollections* are very different from the Alfoxden and Grasmere Journals, and *My Second Tour in Scotland* shows different strategies again. *A Tour on the Continent*, 1820, already reveals some differences in approach but *My Second Tour in Scotland* is much more novelistic – I do not mean this as disparaging, quite the reverse – I am excited by an almost Austenian feel – the Austen, that is, of *Sanditon*, who is alert to changing manners and the personal idiosyncrasies of the people she meets, aware, too, of how the superficies of fashion were changing the face of the country and the people who travelled in it. There is much more dialogue in this 1822 account; there is a much larger number of people, such as travellers in public transport we must meet and of whom we are given casual but revealing snapshots: 'a young Doctor from Glasgow, a writer's clerk, and a widow from Falkirk with a smart daughter' (2, 351). These travellers in turn tell tales, some tall, but many really funny – like the Doctor's story of Dr Swan of Dumbarton who would never give an opinion, but would whisper it into the ears of his mare Susy ('"Shoosy" as the young Doctor pronounced it') as he left the patient: 'Many a death warrant has been pronounced in Shoosy's ears' (2, 352). Rob Roy's cave has become a tourist trap with a venerable Highlander, a Piper and 'boys at different heights with bags of fresh-gathered nuts' (2, 354).

And so, the generic change in Dorothy Wordsworth's writing is intimately bound up with a change in Scotland and the Highlands of Scotland in particular, a change wrought at least in part by the transformation of the Trossachs after the *Lady of the Lake*. Before 1810 there were those 'inhabited solitudes' which Dorothy Wordsworth so brilliantly celebrates as she characterises both the land and its inhabitants and these 'inhabited solitudes' were fit for poetry and for a prose, like Dorothy's, that filled the necessary silences of poetry, thus providing a kind of broad hinterland for poetry. After 1810 the Highlands had become a land fit for the nineteenth-century novel with all that novel's clash and intermingling of culture and opinion. It is perhaps a pity that Dorothy Wordsworth never wrote such a novel, but it is not a pity that she was unable to shape, or deform, her *Recollections* into tourist fodder.

It is, therefore, fitting that the complete text of the *Recollections* should have remained in private circulation until after Dorothy Wordsworth's death. By 1874 Shairp's edition could provide a moving, yet lively, afterlife for Dorothy Wordsworth as well as an elegy for a way of life that had been completely, some would say irreparably, transformed. When Dorothy Wordsworth reached her larger public in Shairp's edition in 1874, she was very well received and it is pleasant to report that most admiring reviewers quoted some part of her adventures in the ferryman's hut on Loch Katrine.

Notes

1   A few sentences from Dorothy Wordsworth's journal of the 1803 tour appear in William Wordsworth's 'Memorials of a Tour in Scotland in 1803', and the memoirs of William published by his nephew the bishop of Lincoln contain extracts from the journal, but the first publication of the whole journal was Shairp's edition in 1874: Dorothy Wordsworth, *Recollections of a Tour made in Scotland, AD 1803*, edited by J. C. Shairp (Edinburgh: Edmiston and Douglas, 1874). All quotations in this article are, however, from de Selincourt's two-volume edition of Dorothy Wordsworth's journals. De Selincourt uses the same manuscript version of the recollections as Shairp but corrects a few mistranscriptions: *Journals of Dorothy Worsdworth*, edited by E. de Selincourt, 2 vols. (London: Macmillan, 1941). References to this edition in the text cite volume and page numbers.

2   See Carol Skyros Walker, *Breaking Away: With Coleridge in Scotland* (New Haven, Conn.: Yale University Press, 2002).

3   *Recollections of the Table Talk of Samuel Rogers*, ed. Morchard Bishop (London: Richards Press, 1952), p. 205.

4   John Stoddart, *Remarks on Local Scenery and Manners in Scotland during the Years 1799 and 1800*, 2 vols. (London: W. Miller, 1801), vol. 1, p. viii.

5   *The Letters of William and Dorothy Wordsworth*, 2 ed., 8 vols. (Oxford: Clarendon Press, 1967–1993), vol. 4, p. 180.

6   *Letters*, vol. 4, p. 104.

7   *Letters*, vol. 1, p. 421.

8   *Letters*, vol. 2, p. 163.

9   Quoted in Mary Moorman, *William Wordsworth: A Biography; the Later Years, 1803–1850* (Oxford: Clarendon Press, 1965), p. 259, note.

Rethinking Scott, his literary predecessors and the imagery of the Highlands

MURDO MacDONALD

Scott's description of the stag in *The Lady of the Lake*, is much more challenging then the image of Landseer's *Monarch of the Glen*. He refers to 'the antlered monarch of the waste', a far more appropriate creature of the upper reaches of Glen Artney where Canto I of *The Lady of the Lake* begins. The problem is that Scott and Landseer have become too closely associated; they have become a conjoined stereotype of the Highlands from which neither can escape. That is not such a problem for Landseer; indeed, without his association with Scott he would be much less known today. But it is a problem for Scott and the Highlands, because Landseer's image of *The Monarch of the Glen* has been visually conflated with Scott's literary work in the minds of so many.

There are, of course, visual alternatives for Scott in a Highland context. Just as earlier chapters have identified other literary triggers for tourist interest in the Highlands, so the response of artists to Highland geography and culture was established well before Scott wrote *The Lady of the Lake*, not least with respect to the work of his two literary predecessors, James Macpherson and Robert Burns. Consider, for example, the etchings and murals produced by Alexander Runciman in response to Macpherson's *Ossian* in the 1770s. This was pioneering Romantic art, developed in the age of neoclassicism by a Scottish artist, trained in Rome and responding to Highland material that had taken Europe by storm. We need to take this wider history of Highland imagery into account. When we do so, we can give value not only to Scott as an author who strongly facilitated the imagery of the Highlands, but also give value to the influence of those who blazed the trail for him.

Since I began by knocking one English artist, Sir Edwin Landseer, off his Scott-related pedestal, let us immediately reinstate another English artist as an interpreter of Scott. J. M. W. Turner is a far greater artist than Landseer and, indeed, an artist capable of matching Scott's own greatness, so, from the point of view explored here, an artist of far more interest than

Landseer. What is of particular importance is that Turner did not simply produce images related to themes in Scott, he produced numerous images made with the specific intention of being reproduced, as engravings, in books by Scott and within Scott's lifetime. These include works such as *Loch Katrine*, a watercolour image Turner finished in about 1832, that was engraved by William Miller in 1833 and published in 1834 as the frontispiece of a new edition of *Lady of the Lake*. And it is important to note the extent of Turner's work here. He produced numerous watercolours in response to Scott's works. In total there were about one hundred images, about eighty of which were made in the 1830s.

There were earlier links between the artist and the writer, in particular for the *Provincial Antiquities* in the 1820s, but the really important collaboration between Turner and Scott started in 1831, the year before Scott's death, when Turner contributed to the new edition of the *Poetical Works*, thanks to being commissioned to do so by Scott's Edinburgh publisher, Robert Cadell. Turner continued to make work for Cadell's editions of Scott after the author's death in 1832. The relationship between Turner and Scott in the writer's final years is of real importance. Turner's image of Melrose, for example, shows not only Scott, but his publisher Cadell and possibly Turner himself in the foreground, picnicking in one of Scott's favourite sites. The thing to note is Turner's interest in Scott himself as part of the landscape, and by extension the landscape as an essential part of Scott. Typically for Turner, it shows the place and the man; it is not only a response to the written word. One might call it total illustration.

Turner knew very well that Scott was dying, and that knowledge seems to have given an edge and an empathy to his images for the *Poetical Works*. They come together into a moving visual tribute to Scott through the places that were significant to him. Consider, for example, an image of a key location for Scott and, indeed, the place where he was buried, Dryburgh. It has an elegiac quality. It was carried out most probably in 1832, engraved by William Miller in 1833 and appeared as the frontispiece to *Sir Tristrem* published as part of the *Poetical Works* in 1834. Thus Turner had finished the image while Scott was still alive, but engraving and publication did not take place until after his death. There is much else to be said about the Turner-Scott relationship: an absorbing account of it can be found in Gerald Finley's 1980 *Landscapes of Memory*.[1] Certainly, of all Turner's images relating to literary subjects – among them illustrations of Byron, Milton and Thomas Campbell – Turner's work for Scott in the 1830s stands out in its intimacy of engagement with both the author and his works. These images of Turner required the highest level of steel engraving, and they found it in the art of, in particular, William Miller, the Edinburgh engraver whom Ruskin later wrote of as Turner's best engraver. Bearing in mind that Miller was an Edinburgh man, and that when he engraved these works in 1833 Scott had just died, he would have felt a keen responsibility to do his best not only for Turner, but for Scott, and indeed he did so.

Turner's travels in the Highlands in pursuit of appropriate imagery for Scott also led to one of his most important full-scale oil paintings, *Staffa, Fingal's Cave*. This was painted in 1832 and Turner leaves one in thoughtful contact with a place rather than in possession of a stereotype. That is, of course, one of the underlying links between Turner and Scott, both were profoundly concerned with the spirit of place rather than with a simple verisimilitude. Like Scott, Turner is sensitive to spirit of place wherever that place may be. Thus in an Italian context he painted *The Golden Bough* and in a Scottish context he painted *Staffa, Fingal's Cave*. They both date from the 1830s. His painting of *The Golden Bough* went on to serve as a stimulus to Sir James Frazer, but it also serves to further illuminate his contribution to Scott, for so many of Turner's works for Scott were not Highland or even Scottish in reference; they were European. An image *Brussels* is a case in point. It was made for Scott's *Life of Napoleon*. Again it was engraved by William Miller. Turner's work for Scott thus ensures that we remember Scott's role as a European writer not just as a commentator on the Highlands or indeed Scotland. If we see Scott through these images his European dimension is emphatic.

It is interesting to recall here that in 1825 Scott dined – and took a considerable interest in – one of Napoleon's former senior military commanders, Marshal Macdonald, who was on the way to visit his father's birthplace in South Uist. Napoleon's enthusiasm for *Ossian* is well known, but whether he associated that work with his senior commander of Highland origin is unknown, or at least not known to me. It is however, worth noting that the very factors which led Macpherson to write *Ossian* in English, were the very factors that led Napoleon to have a senior commander with a Gaelic-speaking father, who himself seems to have had some Gaelic. I refer of course to the Battle of Culloden and the cultural suppression that followed it.

So, if we do wish to see Scott through the eyes of an artist from south of the Border, let it be primarily through the eyes of a great European like Turner. That is not to demean Landseer, he was, after all, one of the finest animal painters of his day, but we must see his contribution in context, for if we do not, the *Monarch of the Glen* stereotype will continue to limit our perception not just of Scott, but of Scotland. Rejecting that stereotype enables us to explore the fact that Scott has a claim to being the greatest European writer of his day, just as Turner has a claim to being the greatest European visual artist. The conjunction between these two men is an extraordinarily important moment in the cultural history of the nineteenth century, which deserves much more recognition as such. It was as a result of his journeying to illustrate Scott's *Lord of the Isles*, that Turner was inspired to paint Staffa. The actual frontispiece he made for the poem was of Loch Coruisk, given as Loch Coriskin, in Skye, and the remarkable watercolour from which it was engraved can be found in the collection of the National Gallery of Scotland. But Turner was not just creating frontispieces. As we have seen he was also making outstanding title page vignettes. For example, opposite the Loch Courisk image was a vignette in which Turner shows Fingal's Cave from it interior.[2]

I have already drawn attention to the importance of Macpherson's *Ossian* in creating the conditions for imagery of the Highlands, so a point to emphasise here is that Turner's Staffa works also of course resonate – in the reference to Fingal – with the work of Macpherson. Macpherson's *Ossian*, published in the 1760s,[3] was not a new interest for Turner. He first toured in Scotland as early as 1799 and one of his earliest recorded Scottish works, dating from 1802, refers to *Ossian*. That landscape is now untraced but it was a view of the Ben Lomond range which had the subsidiary title *The Traveller – Vide Ossian's War of Caros*.[4] There is thus no doubt that Turner's initial reference point for Highland landscape was the work of James Macpherson. Arguably we should regard Turner's Staffa painting from 1832 as owing as much to James Macpherson as to Sir Walter Scott.

The second quarter of the nineteenth century was a time when Turner's ability to produce illustrations for Scott's publisher was helping to drive the art of steel engraving forward, with all the consequences that had for increased print runs of illustrated editions. Note that Turner's steel-engraved Scott illustrations mark a significant increase in the availability of Highland imagery, simply because the durability of the steel plate enables more copies to be made. The many engravings that William Miller made after Turner, included not only *Dunstaffnage* and *Dryburgh* but in 1834 a remarkable image of *Glencoe*. That was published as a frontispiece for another of the volumes of Scott's prose works.[5] Turner's stormy, jagged, exaggerated view of the glen is, one might argue again, as much inspired by Macpherson as by Scott. Although influential at the time – not least on the young Scottish painter, Horatio McCulloch – Turner's radical experimental vision is still not sufficiently appreciated today with respect to the Highlands. I emphasise *Ossian* here to remind the reader again that in any analysis of Scott, to forget James Macpherson is a mistake, for *Ossian* is one of the foundation works of modern European literature and Macpherson prepared the ground for the reception of Scott. In this context, one might consider a pioneering image that begins to make Macpherson's dream Highland landscape a reality and opens up another pathway of literary/artistic influence. This is *Cascade Near Carril* by Charles Cordiner. Published in 1780, it shows Ossian in the foreground. Cordiner, who was minister at Banff, was a key figure in the development of the antiquarian tradition in Scotland, a tradition to which Scott was to make so much contribution in due course.[6] A number of Cordiner's images, including *Cascade Near Carril* were engraved by the London-based firm of Basire.[7] James Basire was an important engraver of antiquities, and the teacher of William Blake. And Blake was, in due course, an *Ossian* enthusiast. It is possible that he saw Cordiner's images towards the end of his apprenticeship with Basire, which ended in 1779. He may even have worked on the plates.[8]

Where Macpherson's geographical references are elusive, those of Scott are precise. It is illuminating to bring Robert Burns into the discussion at this point. Burns's works acted as a stimulus to artists to explore the actual detail of the Highlands in a literary context. In due course this current of activity was developed by artists working with respect to Scott. Some of the earliest landscape illustrations of Burns are of Foyers near Loch Ness, a key stopping point on Burns's Highland tour of 1787. It is no accident that these are by one of Burns's close friends – namely Alexander Nasmyth – an artist described by David Wilkie as the father of Scottish landscape, although most famous today for his portrait of the poet. In images dating from 1803 he was one of the very first artists to provide landscape responses to Burns. The engravers of Nasmyth's images, James Storer and John Greig, were artists in their own right and Greig's illustrations to Burns published along with Nasmyth's in 1805 are among the finest of all responses to the poet.

We can think of Storer and Grieg's Burns illustrations, which are copper plate engravings, as some of the first widely available images of the Highlands, but because they were copper plate engravings they were not as durable as the steel engravings to come via Turner. Nevertheless, the publication of those engravings illustrating Burns in 1805 is a crucial moment in the development of Highland imagery. It gives context not least to painting strongly influenced by Scott, by Alexander Naysmyth's pupil, John Knox. His work *Tourists at Loch Katrine* is, of course, very relevant for us in the context of this volume's themes. It dates from about 1820 and may well not have been painted had it not been for the publication of *The Lady of the Lake*. However it should be pointed out that it could have been, for Knox was a visual explorer of the Highlands just as Scott was a literary explorer. What is interesting for us here is when these two media come together, as in this image.

Knox, through works such as this and his panoramas from Ben Lomond prepared the way for the next generation of Scottish artists that included both Knox's student, Horatio McCulloch, and another important interpreter of the Highlands, D. O. Hill. McCulloch's interpretation of Loch Katrine in 1866 is of interest here, for he has learned much from both Knox and Nasmyth, but his drive towards realistic portrayal is much clearer. Part of that is that he is painting in the full knowledge of that quintessentially Scottish science of the day, namely geology. One can also note that although McCulloch's work is a full-scale oil painting, he owes a great deal to Turner's conception of Loch Katrine made on a much smaller scale to illustrate Scott's *Poetical Works*. It is interesting to note, therefore, that we find McCulloch's image being driven not directly by Scott, but by Turner's response to Scott and that again underlines the importance of giving Turner due regard. This is not to deny the potentially direct influence of Scott on McCulloch, it is just to give it a wider visual context. With respect to the direct influence of Scott on McCulloch one can note that it was McCulloch's brother-in-law, the writer Alexander Smith, who made the often repeated comment that 'Scotland is Scott-land'.

Turner's exploration in the 1830s was of this 'Scott-land'. It is important to make the point again that, because they are steel engravings made for popular editions of Scott, these landscape works of the Highlands by

Turner would have been among the most widely distributed images of the Highlands from the 1830s onwards. So twenty years before Landseer painted *Monarch of the Glen* the most widely distributed images relating to Scott were experimental landscapes by the most experimental painter in Europe. To put it another way, these interpretations of Scott were on the cutting edge of the contemporary art of the day. I suspect that the words 'Scott' and 'cutting edge contemporary art' rarely appear in the same sentence, but I suggest that it is clear that this conjunction makes excellent sense in this context.

This interaction reflects a theme of this chapter, as of this volume, that influential as Scott was, he was part of a wider group of, often interdependent, writers and artists revisioning the Highlands. It is interesting, given this, to compare Turner's – to use again Alexander Smith's term – 'Scottland' with another visual art project from later in the same decade, this time responding to Burns. This was D. O. Hill's *Land of Burns* project which was published in 1840. Hill had also contributed images to the *Prose Works* of Scott, alongside Turner, so there are direct connections here, and, if we are really trying to understand the evolution of imagery of the Highlands, we need to look at visual interpretations of Burns and Scott together, with an awareness of Macpherson as a background. Many of Hill's views for *The Land of Burns* show Highland scenes such as *The Falls of Foyers* and a number were also engraved by the great William Miller, for example, *Loch Turrit*. All refer directly to Burns travels or writings. For example *The Falls of Bruar*, refers directly to Burns's poetical observation to the Duke of Atholl that more trees were needed, and by the time Hill made this image, they had indeed been planted. A few years later, Hill distinguished himself as a pioneer of photography in partnership with Robert Adamson. In passing one can note that our first actual photographic records of Highlanders come courtesy of Hill and Adamson in the 1840s.

There is another Burns illustration that brings Scott strongly to mind. It is an imaginary view of the Highlands by Horatio McCulloch from 1861. In its painted form it was originally entitled *An Emigrant's Dream of His Highland Home*, but, as engraved by William Forrest, it was published as an illustration to Burns's song *My heart's in the Highlands*.[9] Burns's lines, 'My heart's in the Highlands, my heart is not here, / My heart's in the Highlands, a-chasing the deer,' again remind us how important it is to recognise Burns's role in developing imagery of the Highlands in a way we might be more inclined to ascribe to Scott. And those lines of course predate Scott by a generation. As Meg Bateman has pointed out,[10] Burns is not so much constructing a romanticised view here but picking up on Gaelic sentiment, for such a desire to be in the Highlands forms the subject of many a Gaelic song, from the seventeenth century to the present.

The connection of Burns's influence with Scott is not just by analogy. That engraving was published in a portfolio of Burns illustrations under the auspices of the Royal Association for the Promotion of Fine Arts in Scotland, a body closely associated with the Royal Scottish Academy and dedicated to linking art and literature at a high level. These print collections, normally numbering eight prints each, were bound up into portfolios for subscribers and they had print runs of at least five thousand.[11] These were produced from the 1850s to the 1870s. For the first ten years the key author was Robert Burns, but in due course many of Scott's poems and novels were the subjects of these portfolios For example, McCulloch's *Inverlochy Castle* painted in 1857 was engraved for *A Legend of Montrose* in 1877. This is not the place to discuss these portfolios in detail, but their existence underlines the point that I have only space in the context of this volume to scratch the surface of my topic. It is important to see imagery related to Scott in a wider context than is normally the case.

In conclusion, let me draw attention to an example of the complex interactions of relationship and influence we have been exploring in this chapter. This example arises in Scott's own lifetime and reminds us again of James Macpherson's attempt, in *Ossian*, to rehabilitate Gaelic culture in the years of ethnocide after Culloden. An intriguing title page image by Lizars of Edinburgh,[12] for Alexander Campbell's *Albyn's Anthology*, 'a collection of predominantly Highland melodies' published in 1816, shows an iconography that is equally appropriate to either Macpherson or to Scott, namely a deerhound, a red deer stag and, crucially, in the background, the instrument of the bard, the clarsach or harp. Scott was a contributor and Campbell had been Scott's long-suffering music teacher in Edinburgh. Campbell was born by Loch Lubnaig beneath Ben Ledi, that is to say at the heart of the geography and topography that Scott explores in *The Lady of the Lake*. I suggest this is a significant connection. So, this chapter ends, not with a simple conclusion about landscape and Scott, but by noting the need for much more visual research with respect to Scott, this time not only with respect to landscape both Highland and European, but with respect to the iconography of the bard. That is a whole other area that can extend and give context to our perception of Scott in his true relation to, among others, both James Macpherson and Robert Burns.

Notes

1 Gerald Finley, *Landscapes of Memory: Turner as illustrator to Scott* (London: Scolar, 1980).
2 Engraved in this case not by Miller but by Edward Goodall.
3 The two books that constitute *Ossian*, 'Fingal' and 'Temora' were published originally in 1762 and 1763 respectively.
4 Andrew Wilton, *J. M. W. Turner: His Art and Life* (New York: Rizzoli International Publications, 1979), p. 339. [Catalogue of watercolours, no. 346. Untraced (probably a watercolour). Exhibited in the library of the Royal Academy, London, 1802.]
5 Turner's work is probably 1833, Miller's engraving is 1836. See Wilton, p. 443.
6 Charles Cordiner, *Antiquities of the North of Scotland in a Series of Letters to Thomas Pennant* (London: independently published, 1780).
7 Cordiner also takes a strong interest in Pictish work. In one intriguing image a tartan-clad Highlander leans on a Ross-shire Pictish stone in a monument at Sandwick, Ross-shire. That image bears interesting comparison with the title page of volume one of Francis Grose, 1797, *The Antiquities of Scotland*, London: Hooper & Wigstead.
8 Murdo MacDonald, 'The Visual Preconditions of Celtic Revival Art in Scotland', *Journal of the Scottish Society for Art History*, vol. 13, 'Highlands' issue (2008–2009), pp. 16–21.
9 Horatio McCulloch, 1860, 'My Heart's in the Highlands', Edinburgh: Royal Association for the Promotion of Fine Art in Scotland.
10 Meg Bateman, personal communication.
11 My thanks to Dr Joanna Soden of the Royal Scottish Academy for this information.
12 My thanks to John Purser for drawing it to my attention.

Jules Verne and the Trossachs: experience and inspiration

IAN THOMPSON

> He turned one last time to bid goodbye to those magnificent land-
> scapes whose sublime beauty defies the imagination.

These words were penned by Jules Verne recording his first visit to The
Trossachs on the 30 August, 1859 in *Backwards to Britain*.[1] Twenty years
later, on the 16 July 1879, Verne once more gazed on Loch Katrine, accompanied by his son, a nephew and some friends. In addition to revisiting the
landscapes that had so moved him in 1859, added nostalgia was given to his
return for he had recently published one of his most famous novels, set very
largely in The Trossachs.[2]

Verne's first visit, when aged 31, was virtually accidental. At this time
he was living in Paris, having completed a law degree but determined on a
literary career rather than returning to his native city of Nantes to join his
father's legal practice. He married a young widow with two daughters and
although notionally earning a living as a bank dealer, his literary ambitions
were undimmed and he had made the acquaintance of numerous like
spirits in the literary, theatre and musical worlds. Amongst this coterie was
Aristide Hignard, a friend from Nantes since schooldays who was pursuing
a musical career in Paris. Hignard's brother was a shipping agent who
regularly chartered vessels to export French produce to Britain. He was thus
able to offer a free passage to Liverpool to Hignard and he in turn invited
Verne to accompany him. Verne agreed with alacrity since his destination
was not Liverpool but to use this port as a stepping stone to journey on by
train to Edinburgh. This visit was a dream fulfilled for he claimed descent
on his mother's side from a Scottish archer in the service of King Louis XI
of France. Moreover, he was a passionate admirer of Sir Walter Scott. In an
interview with a journalist in 1895 he extolled

> All my life I have delighted in the works of Sir Walter Scott, and
> during a never-to-be-forgotten tour in the British Isles, my happiest
> days were spent in Scotland. I still see as in a vision, beautiful

> picturesque Edinburgh, with its Heart of Midlothian, and many entrancing memories; the Highlands, world-forgotten Iona, and the wild Hebrides. Of course, to one familiar with the works of Scott, there is scarce a district of his native land lacking some association connected with the writer and his immortal work.[3]

During his brief visit to Edinburgh he was befriended by the manager of the city's branch of the City of Glasgow Bank, William Bain, whose daughter prepared an itinerary for a rapid visit to the Highlands. He also met at the Bain's house in Inverleith Row, a catholic priest, William Smith, who ultimately became the Archbishop of St Andrews and Edinburgh and whose brother owned a magnificent mansion in Fife near Oakley which the priest declared would make an excellent starting point for the trip. Miraculously, the handwritten itinerary has survived and is the only known original document recording Verne's 1859 visit.[4]

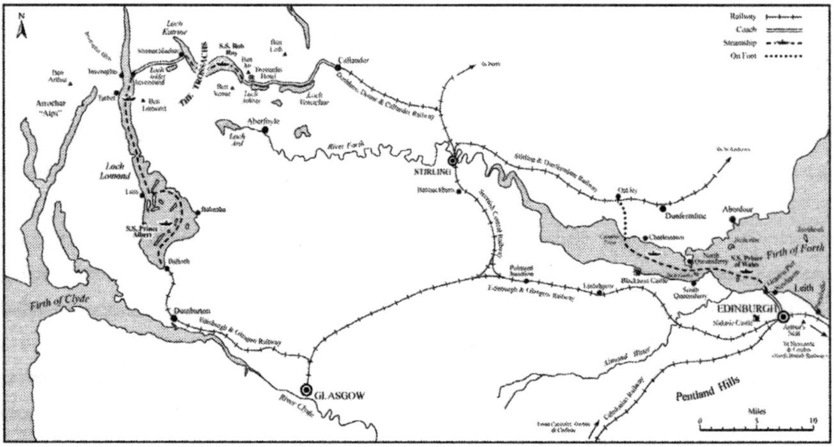

Map © Ian Thompson, 2012. Cartography by Mike Shand.

On the morning of Monday August 29, Verne and Hignard set sail on the *Prince of Wales* steamer from Granton in the teeth of a gale and were put ashore perilously at Crombie Point. Here they were met by the priest and walked across the fields to Inzievar House, the Smith family mansion, where they were given a gargantuan lunch. The two friends then took the train from Oakley station via Stirling to Glasgow Queen Street, staying overnight at the Royal Hotel on George Square. After a brief exploration of the city the next morning, they caught the train to Balloch as the first leg of their Highland excursion. At Balloch they caught the Loch Lomond steamer, the *Prince Albert* and with Ben Lomond emerging through the rain, Verne regaled his companion with tales of the battle of Rob Roy MacGregor against the Colquhoun family. They disembarked at Inversnaid and after a whisky at the inn, mounted the coach for the journey to Stronachlachar, Verne remarking on the grandeur of the view of the Arrochar Alps to the west. At Stronachlachar, the little steamer the *Rob Roy*⁵ awaited them on Loch Katrine. At once Verne's imagination ran riot as he recounted to his companion the legendary deeds of Rob Roy set in a landscape populated by goblins and fairies and immortalised in *The Lady of the Lake*. Landing at The Trossachs pier, once more Verne clambered aboard a coach, this time headed for Callander and thence by train to Stirling to stay overnight at The Golden Lion Hotel before proceeding to Edinburgh and an overnight train to London.

Thus ended Verne's first visit to The Trossachs, but the memory was to remain fresh in his mind and almost twenty years later, in 1877, he was to set one of his most famous novels, *Les Indes noires*, in the Trossachs. The action takes place under Loch Katrine, where the discovery of abundant coal in an abandoned mine leads to the creation of an underground city around a lake, Lake Malcolm. It is a story of good and evil, light and dark, rational and supernatural, a villain and a heroine. The plot is full of twists and turns and the main characters are a former mining family, Simon and Madge Ford and their son Harry, who have remained underground on the closure of the mine. They are joined by the former mine manager, James Starr and a mysterious young girl Nell, who has been rescued deep underground by Harry. Two further characters play an important role in the plot. A demented old man Silfax, who it transpires is Nell's grandfather, and his constant companion, a giant snowy owl. The young Nell has lived all her life underground and it is decided that once her eyes are strong enough she will see the real world. Accordingly the characters embark on a trip via Edinburgh and Glasgow based exactly on Verne's own journey in 1859, with Loch Katrine playing a major role in the denouement. Silfax explodes the roof of the cavern and Loch Katrine drains into it, leaving the travellers aground in the *Rob Roy*. It is evident that Nell and Harry Ford have become enamoured, but on the day of the marriage, the old Silfax appears in a boat on Lake Malcolm with his owl and consumed with anger at the loss of the mine and his granddaughter, sends the owl with a lighted wick to explode the firedamp in the roof of the cavern. Nell calls to the owl, which drops the wick into the lake and flies to her feet. In an act of suicide Silfax jumps into the lake and is drowned. Thus ends an astonishing novel, set in a utopian underground society but in which evil is never far away.[6]

Ironically, Verne set his coalfield in a geologically impossible location. This is readily explained by the fact that he needed an area of outstanding beauty, an atmosphere of supernatural beings and a major lake which after shattering earth movements would flood into the coalfield. The result is a novel of great imagination, yet grounded in Verne's own experience of The Trossachs and inspired by his own perception of Scotland and the Scots. Nevertheless, Verne turns a blind eye to the far from utopian existence of Scottish mining in the nineteenth century, which involved the exploitation not only of men, but of women and young children too. In fact Verne had never entered a Scottish mine and his technical knowledge was derived from a visit to a mine at Anzin in Northern France.[7]

At the time of his first visit, Verne was an unknown author, living in Paris and making a precarious living from work as a librettist, casual work in a bank and the resources of his wife. How different was his return in 1879, as a world-famous author and travelling in his own steam yacht, the *St Michel III*, with a crew of ten. Verne was accompanied by his son Michel and his nephew Gaston, by a close friend Godfroy and by his publisher's son Louis-Jules Hetzel who arrived by train at Edinburgh.[8] In the early hours of Saturday 12 July 1879, the *St Michel* struggled in heavy seas into the port of Leith after a rough crossing from France.[9] Whereas we have limited documentary evidence of the detail of the 1859 visit, in the case of the 1879 return we have the remarkable survival of Verne's *carnet de voyages*, the diary of his voyages in the *St Michel*. We can thus follow his travels on land and sea on a daily basis and practically hour by hour.[10] Verne revisited his haunts in Edinburgh, but, by July 16, he was ready to set off on a journey which was to terminate at the place in Scotland which most enchanted him – the island of Staffa and Fingal's Cave.[11] However, before embarking on this maritime adventure, which was to result in his novel *Le Rayon vert* (*The Green Ray*),[12] he was determined to renew his acquaintance with The Trossachs and Loch Lomond and to show their beauty to his family and friends.

The party left by train from Waverley station to Callander and by coach to Trossachs Pier where the *Rob Roy* was still plying her trade. From Stronachlachar, Verne repeated his coach ride of 1859, but in the opposite direction. At Inversnaid, Verne records his pleasure in seeing the waterfall adjacent to the hotel that he had admired twenty years earlier. From Inversnaid pier, Verne once more embarked on Loch Lomond. The steamer paused at Luss pier and Verne's diary records that here was where he situated 'Malcolm Castle', the starting point of his novel *Les Enfants de capitaine Grant* (*The Children of Captain Grant*),[13] a circumnavigation of the globe in search of a missing Scottish sea captain. 'Malcolm Castle' we can identify as being based on Rhosdhu House, the stately home of the Colquhoun Clan. Disembarking at Balloch, Verne and his companions continued by train to Glasgow and, a creature of habit, Verne booked them once more into the Royal Hotel on George Square. Thus ended Verne's second visit to The Trossachs, Loch Katrine and Loch Lomond. His Scottish journey was to continue by his favoured form of transport, boat, from Glasgow via the Crinan Canal and on to a circumnavigation of Mull with landings at Iona and Staffa before returning by train to Edinburgh and setting sail for France.

Conclusions

What did the Trossachs and Loch Katrine mean to Verne? After all, he spent only a few hours there on each of his two journeys to Scotland.

Firstly, his 1859 visit was his first encounter with mountains and lakes. Born in Nantes, then studying in Paris and marrying a woman from Picardy, Verne had seen nothing more spectacular than rolling chalk hills. His experience of mountains, in ominous and forbidding weather, and steeped in legend and supernatural beings, excited his creative instincts and led directly to his choice of The Trossachs for the locale of *The Underground City*.

Secondly, after his 1859 exploration of Edinburgh's Royal Mile, redolent of *The Heart of Midlothian*, Loch Katrine was his second direct exposure to the locations of the work of Walter Scott, the heartland of Rob Roy country and the setting of *The Lady of the Lake*. We know that Verne was familiar with the work for, in *The Underground City*, one of the principal characters, James Starr, exclaims

> What must not be forgotten is that it served as a theatre for the
> exploits of The Lady of the Lake. I am certain that if our friend Jack

was to look closely, he would see the faint ghost of the beautiful
Ellen Douglas still gliding under its surface.[14]

Thirdly, the two visits saw Verne in different vein. On his first visit
he was a young man with a mission, to explore 'his' Scotland, to inhale
its scenery, history and culture and to absorb the personality of the Scot.
When he returned twenty years later, he was mature, less excitable and more
financially secure. He was therefore almost a genuine tourist, determined
to show the beauty of Loch Katrine and The Trossachs to his travelling
companions. The impact of this, and his other Scottish experiences, resulted
in five works set entirely or partially in Scotland, in addition to the autobiographical account of his 1859 visit, *Backwards to Britain*, and no less than
forty Scottish characters populate his total literary output. *The Green Ray*
commences on the Gareloch near Helensburgh and involves a frustrating
search for the elusive green ray, the sight of which is held to confirm the
discovery of true love. This search on the part of a young woman involves
a traverse of Argyll by steamer and reaches its climax in Fingal's Cave on
the Isle of Staffa. As already indicated, the action of *The Underground City*
is situated almost entirely on and below Loch Katrine. Two books in which
the main characters are Scots commence and end in Scotland. *Les forceurs
de blocus* (*The Blockade Runners*)[15] is an action-packed novella involving the
forcing of the Northern blockade of the Confederate port of Charleston,
South Carolina, during the American Civil War. *The Children of Captain
Grant* begins on the Clyde, when the wealthy aristocrat Lord Glenarvan
discovers a clue, recovered from the stomach of a shark, to the disappear-
ance of a Captain Grant, a Scottish sea captain. Accompanied by his new
wife and by the two children of the missing captain, Glenarvan leaves his
ancestral Castle Malcolm at Luss on Loch Lomond and circumnavigates
the world in his steam yacht, leading to the successful discovery of Captain
Grant. It is one of Verne's longest novels and he loses no opportunity to
extol the virtues of the Scottish character, to the extent that a certain stereo-
typing becomes evident: the patriotic and public-spirited aristocrat, the
dutiful and loyal wife, the respectful children and the qualities of endurance
and seamanship in the crew.

Significantly, we find in these novels an echo of Ellen, the Lady of the Lake.
Verne admitted to his publisher that he had no talent for portraying female
characters, especially in a romantic context, being much more attracted to

what was, in his view, the adventurous potential of men. However, in each of the Scottish novels we find a romantic heroine, portrayed in the most favourable light, and in three cases they are given a name close to Ellen. In *The Children of Captain Grant*, Lord Glenarvan's wife is Lady Helena. In *The Green Ray*, the heroine is Helena Campbell. In *The Underground City*, the 'Child of the Cavern' is called Nell, a diminutive form of 'Helen'.

The Trossachs, along with Edinburgh, most embodied Verne's admiration for Sir Walter Scott and his own distant Scottish roots, but it was the Trossachs that most stimulated his creative imagination and resulted in his most successful Scottish novel, *The Underground City*. It was almost certainly the beauty of Loch Katrine and the drama of Scott's epic poem set there that led him to the observation that 'There is only one nation given by God. That is Scotland to the Scots'.[16]

Notes

1 Jules Verne, *Backwards to Britain*, trans. J. Valls-Russell (Edinburgh: Chambers, 1992) is the English translation of *Voyages à reculons en Angleterre et en Ecossse* (Paris: Le Cherche Midi, 1989). The manuscript was rejected by Verne's publisher and was only rediscovered over a century later. It is clear that, although Verne conceals the identity of himself and some of the people that he met, the book is an autobiographical account of his 1859 journey, with additional material for dramatic or comical effect.

2 Jules Verne, *Les Indes noires* (Paris: Hetzel, 1877).

3 M. Belloc, 'Jules Verne at Home', *Strand Magazine*, February, 1895. For a very detailed account of Verne's travels in Scotland and commentary on his 'Scottish' novels see Ian Thompson, *Jules Verne's Scotland in Fact and Fiction* (Edinburgh: Luath Press, 2011).

4 For an account of the 1859 visit including a reproduction of the handwritten itinerary, see Ian Thompson, 'The visit to Scotland by Jules Verne in 1859', *Scottish Geographical Journal* vol. 121, no. 1 (2005, pp. 103–6).

5 In fact this was the second ship on Loch Katrine to bear the name *Rob Roy*, replacing *Rob Roy I* in 1855. It was jointly owned by the three hotels at Inversnaid, Stronachlachar and the Trossachs – an early example of integrated tourism.

6 Several English language translations with varying titles and quality have been published. The most recent and complete is Jules Verne, *The Underground City*, trans. Sarah Crozier (Edinburgh: Luath Press, 2005).

7 H. Marel, 'Jules Verne, Zola et la mine', in 'Germinal: Une Documentation Intégral', *University of Glasgow French and German Publications* (1989), pp. 248–63.

8 Verne's nephew Gaston inexplicably shot him outside the author's house in 1886. A bullet remained lodged in his foot and Verne was lame for the rest of his life. The motivation has not been conclusively explained, but Gaston remained in mental institutions for the remainder of his life.

9 The arrival of the *St Michel* is recorded in the Leith Port Register, 1879. National Archives of Scotland catalogue number GD229/2/48.

10 For an account of Verne's 1879 visit to Scotland see Ian Thompson, 'The second visit to Scotland by Jules Verne in 1879', *Scottish Geographical Magazine*, vol. 123, no. 3 (2008)

pp. 281–6. The itinerary in the Trossachs follows that indicated on the map shown on p. 134 but was in the reverse direction as compared with 1859.

11 The *carnet de voyage* is housed in the *Bibliothèque Municipale* of Amiens and can be consulted online there.

12 Jules Verne, *Le Rayon vert* (Paris: Hetzel, 1882). This has been translated by Karen Loukes as Jules Verne, *The Green Ray* (Edinburgh: Luath Press, 2009).

13 *Les Enfants du capitaine Grant* (Paris: Hetzel, 1868).

14 The *Underground City*, op. cit., p179.

15 Jules Verne, *Les forceurs de blocus* (Paris: Hetzel, 1872).

16 Jules Verne, *Sans dessus dessous* (Paris: Hetzel, 1889), chapter 2.

Location, dislocation: film and the Trossachs

DAVID MANDERSON

When Trevor Duncan, BBC producer and composer of British light music, spoke about his best-known composition, the March from *Little Suite*, he insisted its source of inspiration was the English countryside.[1] He may have been irritated by the fact that his most famous air had become closely associated with a particular part of, not the English, but the Scottish landscape, so closely linked to it in people's minds, in fact, that the two – the place and the music – were inseparable. As the theme music of *Dr Finlay's Casebook*, one of the most popular early television series during the 1960s,[2] Duncan's composition could be heard in millions of living rooms across the country, the first sound viewers experienced as they watched images intended to encapsulate the series' setting and tone.

The point of theme music, of course, is to become as much a part of a screen drama as the characters, the plots and the place. It announces the fictional universe the viewer is about to enter. Who can listen now to Duncan's theme without thinking of the invented town of Tannochbrae, or of the countryside around it? It may be forty years since *Dr Finlay's Casebook* made its last appearance on the BBC (it was resurrected on ITV more recently, running from 1993 to 1996 and starring David Rintoul, Annette Crosbie and Ian Bannen), and it was not originally written for the series, but it still came to symbolise the lives of Dr Finlay, Dr Cameron, Janet the Housekeeper, Dr Snoddie and the rest. Hearing it, you knew you were about to enter an invented but well known world and a particular place in it.

This chapter looks at the history of film in the Trossachs, using this small area of lochs, woods and mountains as a case study of how film and place are interlinked, successfully or unsuccessfully – although perhaps, in the interests of accuracy, its subject should be the history of the Trossachs on screen, to allow *Dr Finlay's Casebook* and other television series to be included. It concerns screen dramas made in or about the Trossachs, tracing the history of some of stories that filmmakers chose to set here, and their reasons for doing so. As we shall see, there can be many, some obvious, others less so. But what is certain is that the Trossachs can claim to be a major centre of film production. The list of films or television programmes that either feature it strongly as a location or use it as a single location among many others is impressive:

- *Rob Roy*: three of the five film versions made of the story used the Trossachs as their location, in 1911, 1922 and 1953.
- *Geordie* (1955): filmed in and around Aberfoyle (see below).
- *The Thirty-Nine Steps*: two of the four film adaptations made of Buchan's book used Trossachs locations, in 1959 and 2008 (see below).
- *Dr Finlay's Casebook* (1962–71): used Callander for its outdoor locations (see below).
- *Casino Royale* (1967): the spoof Bond film starring Peter Sellers used the Falls of Dochart in Killin as a backdrop in one scene.
- *Monty Python and the Holy Grail* (1975): used the Duke's Pass and Tomnadashan Mine Cave in some of its scenes before moving from the Trossachs to Doune Castle in Stirlingshire.
- *The Last Great Wilderness* (1975): this road movie and thriller also used the Duke's Pass, in this case to represent a wilderness where fugitives are on the run.
- *Take the High Road* (1980–2003): the long-running soap opera, filmed in Luss.
- *Kuch Kuch Hota Hai* (1998): a Bollywood blockbuster, with some sections filmed at Inchmahome Priory.
- *This is not a love song* (2003): filmed around Kinlochard and Loch Katrine (see below).

The 1911 *Rob Roy* starred John Clyde, who had made the part his own on stage, and was produced by United Films on location in Aberfoyle and in studios in Rouken Glen in the south side of Glasgow.[3] The 1922 version made by Gaumont starred David Hawthorne and was directed by W. P. Kellino,[4] while Walt Disney's 1953 *Rob Roy: The Highland Rogue*, starring Richard Todd, is still remembered by many (see below).

Scotland has been visualised extensively in films, and there are other popular film locations in it. Glencoe is one used time and again, for

Hitchcock's famous 1935 version of *The Thirty-Nine Steps* and the *Harry Potter* series among others. But measured against these other areas, the Trossachs has been used as much as any of them, and more than most. One reason is simply its beauty. The tall mountains and deep valleys offer filmmakers the ideal setting for particular kinds of stories. The landscape is part of the spectacle, the composition, the colour and grandeur. Another reason is that filmmakers and their locations scouts, who search out suitable places for films to be made, would be aware of the area through the visual arts, a Romantic tradition passed down through theatrical scene painting and landscape painting,⁵ and originally derived, of course, in great measure from Sir Walter Scott's *The Lady of the Lake* and *Rob Roy*, to photography and cinema. This can, indeed, be seen as a consequence of the relationship of Scott to Turner and other artists discussed by Murdo Macdonald in his chapter in this volume. In fact, the Trossachs can be seen, through tourism, to have come to stand for Romantic Scotland itself. And Walter Scott, the Trossachs and filmmakers crossed over in another way too, which is that all these creators knew about the power of fiction, the empowerment of entertainment, and the importance of an authentic sense of place to it.

The first six episodes of the BBC *Dr Finlay* were, however, not filmed in the Trossachs, but in Milngavie, at Tannoch Loch. But then the series switched its external locations to Callander. Famously, the opening credits of *Dr Finlay* showed scenes of the Trossachs countryside, wooded slopes and misty mountains, including the Red Bridge over the River Teith: a sort of compendium of Scottish images – hills and forests and bubbling rivers – that became in viewers' minds deeply associated with the jaunty tune. All this was carried into the drama by the other things that made up the fiction: the acting, the directing, the costumes, the props, the characters, the dialogue, the plots of each episode, and so on. Tannochbrae seemed like a real place in a real time. We imagined it was still there, everyone going about their business, even when the programme was not being broadcast. And conversely a truly real place, the town of Callander, became firmly fixed in the popular imagination as a piece of fiction.⁶ (In a way, television was only following where literature had already gone, as the fictional village of Tannochbrae was based, in turn, on the fictional town of Levenford in A. J. Cronin's original Dr Finlay novel *A Country Doctor*, which was modelled on the real town of Cardross, Cronin's birthplace.)

The feeling that what we are watching is real happens a great deal in screen drama, especially long-running series. The Rovers Return in *Coronation Street*, the Queen Vic in *Eastenders*, their music, characters, conventions and layouts can seem utterly familiar, places we visit regularly. The fictions are meant to make us believe in them. But we should bear in mind that screen dramas distort real locations more than literary texts, using them for their own ends and choosing how much to reinvent them. When Arthur Freed, the producer of *Brigadoon*, visited Scotland to search for locations, he returned to the States disappointed, claiming he had not found anything particularly Scottish there.[7] And so a mythical Scotland, complete with mists, kilts and dancing Highlanders, was built on a Hollywood film set. Similarly, Cronin's novels, originally set in Dunbartonshire, were switched to the Trossachs on television, and even a home-grown BBC series like *Dr Finlay's Casebook* was mostly made on a set in London, only its external shots being filmed in Callander.

So why take your production to the Trossachs at all? Why not just build your own version of Scotland on a set, or go to somewhere more remote and wild? One answer is very simple. The Trossachs is close to Glasgow. Film production on location means a huge investment of resources. Even the smallest needs many people to produce, market and distribute it. A major feature film involving, say, battle scenes, can use thousands. The cost of all this means that productions have to be kept to the tightest possible schedule, and locations have to be found in advance. If the story involves wilderness, or geographical beauty, or Scottishness, or imagery that we might call in any way romantic, the Trossachs is only an hour's drive away from a major city and a centre of film production. It is convenient. So it is tempting to use it as a location even if your original story – the book or story on which your film is based – was originally set somewhere else.

Just this happened with one of the most famous texts to have passed from books into films. When film was new, and film makers were casting about for stories to make into films, they naturally picked stories that had already proved themselves. They could be so much more hopeful of a hit. So *Dracula, Frankenstein, Jekyll and Hyde* and others including Walter Scott's novels, including *Rob Roy*, were some of the first features made. When John Buchan in 1915 wrote the very first spy thriller – he called it a 'shocker' – he probably did not realise that he was bringing into being a genre that would ultimately lead to Daniel Craig and the James Bond brand. His *The*

Thirty-Nine Steps is really just a chase. A hero gets into trouble – accused unjustly of murder – and has to flee, friendless and alone, but always optimistic and resourceful, pursued by enemies as well as the authorities. A chase requires a wilderness to flee across, preferably exotic. The original Richard Hannay in Buchan's novel sought escape in Galloway because it was remote and 'not over thick with population'.[8] In 1935, Alfred Hitchcock made the most famous of the book's adaptations into film, changing the story freely so that Hannay is no longer South African, but Canadian, and has a female companion as he goes on the run, with the south-western setting becoming Glencoe. It was Hitchcock's most successful picture at that stage of his career, and subsequent adaptations looked back as much to it as to the original book. But they could also change and update elements as they chose. (The 1978 version, however, starring Robert Powell, was the most loyal to the book – despite the claims made for the 2008 television version – and did use the Borders for its locations.)

The 1959 version of *The Thirty-Nine Steps*, directed by Ralph Thomas and starring Kenneth More, used the Trossachs extensively, setting most of its story in and around it. This version dispenses with the World War One context, setting its story in the Cold War era. Kenneth More is the adventurer Hannay, now neither South African nor Canadian, but a well-travelled English diplomat who has recently returned to London. Finding a gun in a pram in Regent's Park, he is drawn into a complex web of spy rings and, wrongly accused of murder, is obliged to flee north. Pursued by the police, he jumps from a train on the Forth Road Bridge (an incident not in the book, but which also takes place in the Hitchcock version) and then, accompanied by a variety of female companions, walks, cycles, hitches lifts and runs from one end of the Trossachs to the other. Locations include the Brig o' Turk tearoom (which is still there) as 'The Gallows Inn' where cyclists gather, the Duke's Pass and the Trossachs Hotel on Loch Ard, now a timeshare holiday development. It is easy to see why the Trossachs was chosen: the exciting tale unfolds against a backdrop of beautiful scenery that changes constantly, although the locations are close to each other, giving the film-makers opportunity for variety of setting without too many changes of location. Hannay hides among a mob of cyclists in the low wooded valley overlooked by Ben A'an, is pursued by the police on high bare summits and chased through trim estate grounds. Later, he saunters past the Falls of Dochart and over the bridge at Balquhidder, retitled 'Glenkirk' in this film.

This version of Buchan's story was a very British affair. Ralph Thomas also directed the *Doctor* series of films and was associated with the *Carry On* series, and his *The Thirty-Nine Steps* has a sort of British jauntiness that is appropriate for Buchan's original story, but also very different from the brooding Hitchcock version. We can see in More's confident swagger, his clothes – the angled trilby and the old-fashioned tweeds made new – his flirtatiousness with the female characters and his facility with weapons, elements that Sean Connery was to carry on into the James Bond movies only a few years later, and which continue today. Other actors involved were recognisable from their appearances in many other British films of the period: they include Brenda de Banzie, Sid James as a lorry driver who gives Hannay a lift, Andrew Cruikshank, Joan Hickson, John Grieve, the ubiquitous Sam Kydd (as a waiter on the train Hannay catches for the mysterious north) and the character actor you sent for then when you wanted a Scottish older man, a father-type, Jameson Clark. In fact, in all films set in Scotland the same character actors tend to appear in similar roles, and it can be interesting to look out for John Laurie, Stanley Baxter, Gordon Jackson, Finlay Currie, Duncan Macrae and others among the village or city types.

It is a pleasure to look at this version of *The Thirty-Nine Steps* and see a place we recognise as it is now, or even more interestingly, as it was, but not all films respect their location in this way. It is possible in films to put two or more different places together to make a fictional one, to pretend they make one place when in reality they are miles apart. Bill Forsyth's *Local Hero* (Forsyth) used the town of Pennan in the east and a beach at Morar in the west to make the fictional town of Ferness, but it was done with loving affection for the world depicted in Forsyth's original script and a concern for its environment, even if it was fictional.[9] Place was at the centre of the story, and it is no accident, but a measure of *Local Hero's* long-term success as a film, that Pennan has continued to be one of the most visited locations in Europe.[10] In 2008, however, another version of *The Thirty-Nine Steps*, this one made for television, also used the Trossachs for some of its locations. Starring Rupert Penry-Jones, Lydia Leonard and Patrick Malahide, it claimed to look back to Buchan's original in ways that earlier adaptations had not.[11] Again, the hero is unjustly accused. Again, he goes on the run in Scotland. Filming took place in Stirling Castle, Dumbarton Castle, Edinburgh (which doubled for London), Kelvingrove Art Gallery (which became St Pancras Station), and Argyll. Locations change suddenly and without warning. There is no relation between one place and the next geographically, and the same sense of dislocation emerges dramatically. Near the end of the film, at its climax, Hannay and his companion, wandering round a gloomy castle, suddenly open a door on a steep flight of computer-generated steps leading down to Brenachoile Lodge on Loch Katrine. They run down the steps only to witness a German submarine surfacing. A gun battle ensues between Hannay and the German spies on the pier. The spot must have been useful for filming – quiet, isolated and with a long stretch of water on which to superimpose the image of the submarine – but it has little relevance to character, narrative or plot. It is an example of a Trossachs setting being used merely as a backdrop, without any link between the story and the real place. It would be a remarkable feat of navigation for a sea-going submarine to make its way into Loch Katrine!

This absence of geographic link is found too in another more recent Trossachs-based production. *This is not a love song*, directed by Bille Eltringham, was released in 2002, the first film to be launched simultaneously in cinemas and on-line. Another thriller involving a chase through a wilderness, in this case the flight of two ex-convicts on the run after accidentally killing a farmer's daughter, it has, like the 2008 version of *The Thirty-Nine Steps*, little relationship to its setting, using the Trossachs as an unidentified setting rather than a real place. Indeed, this film's very use of the Trossachs was accidental. Originally set on the Yorkshire moors using mostly English actors, the film's producers had to change their plans because of the outbreak of foot and mouth disease in 2001. Locations were changed to Inverness but these too fell through. So the Trossachs was eventually selected simply because it was a wild place, an open space of moors, ferns and water where a chase could take place. Shots of anonymous bogs and lochs do not create a sense of any kind of identity of place.

Hard though it is to make any kind of a film anywhere – and so the making of any one in Scotland is to be welcomed – *This is not a love song* and the 2008 version of *The Thirty-Nine Steps* were not especially well-received critically. Does the lack of any real link between location and story affect a film's resonance? Does some kind of emotional truth need to be captured about a place, as well as about characters and relationships, for a film to convince?

Much more successful was the next film under consideration, which is one that has been so thoroughly criticised and reconstructed that it can be hard to evaluate the original. To say it is full of stereotypes is to point out the obvious. It is so stereotypical that what we consider stereotypically Scottish, and why, is called into question. Filmed in and around Balquhidder, Loch Arklet and Loch Ard Forest, far from seeking to change traditional Scottish images it runs towards them and embraces them. The opening moments of *Geordie* (1955), directed by Frank Launder, show the stunning scenery at the head of Loch Voil. As the camera pans across the hills to look down on the schoolhouse a caption reads 'The Place – Scotland. The time – Yesterday and Today. With a wee keek at Tomorrow'. Wee Geordie, played by the ten-year old Paul Young, is running towards his school. The bell in the mellow-stoned school tower is tolling the hour. In the schoolroom, the stern but kindly teacher, played by Duncan Macrae, is quizzing his class on vocabulary. 'Stand up, whoever said that' he orders them. 'Please sir, I am standing up' Wee Geordie says to general laughter. Wee Geordie is laughed at for his stature, creating a sense of shame that will haunt him into adulthood, until he faces the fact that self-esteem and courage are not about physical size. The scenery, the little rural school, the dominie, the sometimes uncertain accents, the collie dog, wee Jeannie waiting on the hill: we can see in these few shots many of the clichés that led later critics, such as those who put together the influential collection of essays *Scotch Reels* in 1982, to attack almost the whole history of the representation of Scotland on screen. In Cairns Craig's words:

> The speech of Lowland Scotland, the landscape of the Highlands have become clichés which need to acquire a new historical significance before they can become released [...] from the frozen worlds of their myths [...][12]

We have, however, become much more interested in these myths in the thirty years since *Scotch Reels* was written, and we can see them now as alive, not frozen. In fact recent study has rather left the *Scotch Reels* debate behind revealing it as limited and sterile, and often based on insecure research. [13] If we watch *Geordie*, originally a novel by an expatriate Scot, Canadian David Walker, as just a story, a charming romance that shows naïve and sentimental affection for a Scotland that had existed in international fiction for many years, and uses a real location as an integral part of its impact on its audience, perhaps we can start to forgive it some of its supposed sins.

Forsyth Hardy, however, argues differently, seeing Geordie's story as '[...] a simple film [... that] could have been placed anywhere, from Poland to Peru'.[14] Bill Travers got into shape for the movie, using bodybuilding to become the athlete he was portraying, the muscle-bound manifestation of his obstinacy.[15] Norah Gorsen as Jean assumed one of the less convincing accents in the history of Scottish film.[16] Character actor Jameson Clark, already referred to, and who also appeared regularly in *Dr Finlay's Casebook*, played Geordie's tragic father, who bequeaths to Geordie his gun and his Black Watch kilt; Molly Urquhart was Geordie's indomitably supportive mother; Stanley Baxter played the part of the postie; while Alasdair Sim brought his real Scottish background to bear on his portrayal of the eccentric and comical laird.

Scotch Reels identified two particularly grave ideological sins, Tartanry and Kailyardism, which it levelled at representations of Scotland with Calvinist zeal.[17] *Geordie* must have seemed particularly guilty in the eyes of these critics since it combined the two. But we can read it too as loyal to its place and time even if that world was largely fictional, and it used the Trossachs in a real way to do it. In the Highland Games scene, a host of supposed stereotypes appear in rapid succession in a way the *Scotch Reels* critics would have seen as pure Scottish kitsch. Small girls dance in full Highland regalia, pipers pipe, caber-throwers toss and beefy laddies whirl the hammer. But the scene was shot in a real place associated with these same elements: in the playing fields of Aberfoyle School, directly in front of the school itself, which can sometimes be seen in the background.

Film in its earliest days looked around for tried and tested stories. It was entirely predictable that Scotland's greatest novelist, Walter Scott, would have many of his books made into films,[18] and only a matter of time before one of film's giants, Walt Disney, turned his attention to Scotland and to Walter Scott's storytelling within it. The Disney corporation made four Scottish films altogether: *Greyfriars Bobby* (1961), *Kidnapped* (1960) and *The Three Lives of Thomasina* (1964) were filmed in Edinburgh, Glencoe and Inveraray respectively. But *Rob Roy: The Highland Rogue* (1953) was probably the most successful.[19] Starring Richard Todd, then a rising star on both sides of the Atlantic, Glynis Johns and James Robertson Justice, the film was a rousing action-filled blockbuster with a cast of thousands. The impact of such a cast is seen, and is impressive, in the opening scene where hundreds of troops march up the hillside, while the Highland host waits in ambush on the mountaintop. At a shout in Gaelic from Rob Roy, the clansmen charge down the steep slopes. The battle sequences are entirely authentic. Most of the filming took place above Kinlochard, where soldiers from the Argyll and Sutherland Highlanders, who had recently returned from the Korean War, were used to recreate the troops on both sides.[20] Legend has it that the battle scenes were the ordinary privates' opportunity to take revenge on their NCOs, and that they took great pleasure in knocking about their tormentors.

Rob Roy: the Highland Rogue is an out-and-out action picture. Rob is captured in the opening scenes, and the rest of the film concerns itself with his adventures in escaping and living on the run, until eventually his brave Highlanders march to Edinburgh, reconcile themselves to King George, and live happily ever after in the heather. There often seems little resemblance between Walter Scott's original novel and the film versions, and no concern at all for historical accuracy. Disney has been accused with some justice of appropriating other cultures, from children's fairy tales to national myths, and there are many reasons to mistrust a corporate commercial approach to story telling. But the Disney Company's employees, like Scott, were marvellous storytellers, and although Scott's version could seem lost, many more elements from the original novel to the film were preserved than seems obvious. One incident in particular survives through all the different versions, from Scott's up to the present day, and it seems also to have been an incident from the real Rob Roy's life. It is the moment where, captured and tied, Rob makes a daring bid for escape as his captors cross a mountain burn. In the 1953 version, the moment of action shows Rob bursting free of his guards, diving deep into the water from his horse to avoid the bullets from the pursuing troops and going over a waterfall before tugging off his bonds with his teeth, and casting off his plaid to deceive the soldiers. It was filmed at the Black Linn of Blairvaich, on the Falls of Douchray between Kinlochard and Aberfoyle, and the filmmakers used the deep pool beyond the falls, the narrow gorge of the river and the rocky outcrops along its banks to create the exciting chase.

There has been so far one more version of *Rob Roy*, but it was not filmed in the Trossachs. The 1995 film, starring Liam Neeson, Jessica Lange, John Hurt, Brian Cox and Tim Roth was filmed in Glencoe, Glen Nevis, Morar and other places. Nevertheless in its spirit it too caught what Scott's original novel was all about, and in that it could also be said to catch the spirit of this area. It is a Trossachs movie in intention, if not in fact. Another dissimilarity points to another difference: the use of Gaelic. In the 1953 film, it is spoken from character to character and from actor to audience, if only occasionally. By 1995, it has become a mournful song, a heritage display, even if expertly performed by Karen Matheson of the band *Capercaillie*. The developments Michael Newton's chapter discusses still need to be addressed.

At the start of this review of film in the Trossachs, we speculated that there might be another reason for the area's popularity in film other than its proximity to Glasgow. That is the way the Trossachs became embedded in popular consciousness as the very embodiment of Scottish Romanticism through the work of Scott. As a tourist area, it was already well known to filmmakers when film was young, and to location scouts if they wanted to set a film here. Through Scott's work people already knew of the magic of this borderland between Highland and Lowland, old religion and new, English and Gaelic, Protestant and Catholic, and they knew of its scenery. It was ready-made to be transferred into a visual medium. And that type of visual storytelling was forming the way people read and saw the world long before films came along. Here is a passage from Scott's *Rob Roy*:

> We arrived at an eminence covered with brushwood, which gave us a commanding prospect down the valley [... The soldiers] had taken up their situation [...] on a rising ground in the centre of the little valley of Aberfoil [...] The appearance of the picqueted horses, feeding in this little vale; the forms of the soldiers as they sate, stood or walked, formed a noble foreground, while far to the eastward the eye caught a glance of the lake of Menteith [...][21]

This is a description we can see, a place we recognise, with movement in it. In short, it is a film shot. We could set up a camera and take it ourselves from any of the hills overlooking Aberfoyle. We may even feel we have stood on the very spot looking over the view Scott describes.

Film-like imagination and visualisation existed long before films were made and long before the birth of cinema Scott was the most filmic of writers. As Richard Butt observes, his work was among the first to be exploited by film.[22] His stories were highly suitable to the new medium when it arrived and easily adaptable to the big screen. Meanwhile, the Trossachs was his most famous set, known all over the world through his writing. That tradition continued unbroken from and through the media of the nineteenth and twentieth centuries into film, where Scott's stories and, even more importantly, the legacy of his romantic influence in the interpretation of the Scottish landscape created a vivid picture of Scotland that this small area seems to entirely contain. That is the legacy of the Trossachs in film today.

Notes

1   T. McDonald and E. Tomlinson, 'Little Suite: March – Trevor Duncan (b. 1924)' CD sleeve note, Elizabethan Serenade: *The Best of British Light Music* (Munich: MVD Music, 1996).
2   Duncan Petrie, *Screening Scotland* (London: British Film Institute, 2000), p. 132.
3   Petrie, p. 18.
4   Petrie, p. 55.
5   Ibid.
6   David Bruce, *Scotland the Movie* (Edinburgh: Polygon, 1996), p. 41.
7   Forsyth Hardy, *Scotland in Film* (Edinburgh: Edinburgh University Press, 1990), p. 1.
8   John Buchan, *The Thirty-Nine Steps*, in *The Complete Richard Hannay* (London: Penguin, 1956), p. 18.
9   Bruce, p. 205.
10 Louise Jury, 'Location, Location, Location: A Movie Buff's Choice', *The Independent*, 23 July 2005.
11 A. A. Gill, 'Rupert Penry-Jones Shines in The 39 Steps', *The Sunday Times*, 4 January 2009.
12 Cairns Craig, 'Myths against History: Tartanry and Kailyard in 19th-Century Scottish Literature' in Colin McArthur (ed.), *Scotch Reels* (London: British Film Institute, 1982), p. 15.
13 The vitality of the current debate is reflected throughout Ian Brown (ed.), *From Tartan to Tartanry: Scottish Culture, History and Myth* (Edinburgh: Edinburgh University Press, 2010), particularly in Brown's own chapter 'Myth, Political Caricature and Monstering the Tartan', pp. 93-114, and Richard Butt, 'Looking at the Tartan in Film: History, Identity and Spectacle', pp. 165–79.
14 Hardy, p. 98.
15 Ibid.
16 Bruce, p. 242.
17 Craig, pp. 7–16.
18 For an interesting discussion of the role of adaptations of Scott throughout the history of screen media, see Richard Butt, 'Literature and the Screen Media since 1908', in Ian Brown *et al.* (eds.), *The Edinburgh History of Scottish Literature* (Edinburgh: Edinburgh University Press, 2007), vol. 3, pp. 53–63.
19 Petrie, pp. 62–4.
20 Hardy, p. 94.
21 Walter Scott, *Rob Roy* (Harmondsworth: Penguin, 1995), pp. 394–5.
22 Butt, 'Literature and the Screen Media', p. 53.

Filmography

- Michael Caton-Jones, *Rob Roy*, United Artists, 1995
- Bille Eltringham, *This is not a love song*, Footprint Films *et al.*, 2002
- Harold French, *Rob Roy: The Highland Rogue*, Disney, 1953
- Bill Forsyth, *Local Hero*, Goldcrest Films, 1983
- James Hawes, *The Thirty-Nine Steps*, BBC, 2008
- Alfred Hitchcock, *The Thirty-Nine Steps*, Gaumont British, 1935
- Karan Johar, *Kuch Kuch Hota Hai*, Dharma Productions, 1998
- Frank Launder, *Geordie*, Individual Pictures, 1955
- Don Sharp, *The Thirty-Nine Steps*, Rank Organisation, 1978
- Ralph Thomas, *The Thirty-Nine Steps*, Rank Organisation, 1959

Bibliography

[Anon], *The Traveller's Guide; or, a Topographical Description of Scotland* (Edinburgh: J. Fairbairn, 1798).

[Anon], *A Sketch of the Most Remarkable Scenery near Callander of Monteath; Particularly the Trossachs* (Stirling: C. Randall, 1800).

[Anon] Glasgow City Archives, MS TD 637/1 *First Tour to the Highlands, 1817* and *[Second Tour] 1818*.

Malcolm Andrews, *The Search for the Picturesque: Landscape, Aesthetics and Tourism in Britain, 1760–1800* (Aldershot: Scolar Press, 1989).

Michael Brander, *A Hunt Around the Highlands* (Gloucester: Standfast Press, 1973).

Barbara Bell, 'The National Drama, Joanna Baillie and the National Theatre', in Ian Brown *et al.* (eds.) *The Edinburgh History of Scottish Literature* (Edinburgh: Edinburgh University Press, 2007) vol. 2, pp. 228–35.

Barbara Bell 'The National Drama and the Nineteenth Century', in Ian Brown (ed.), *The Edinburgh Companion to Scottish Drama* (Edinburgh: Edinburgh University Press, 2011), pp. 47–59.

M Belloc, 'Jules Verne at Home', *Strand Magazine*, February, 1895.

Roger Bilcliffe, *The Glasgow Boys* (London: John Murray, 1984).

Ronald Black (ed.), *An Lasair: Anthology of 18th Century Scottish Gaelic Verse* (Edinburgh: Birlinn Ltd, 2001).

Ronald Black, 'The Gaelic Academy: The Cultural Commitment of the Highland Society of Scotland', *Scottish Gaelic Studies*, 14 (1986), pp. 1–38.

Elizabeth A. Bohls and Ian Duncan (eds.), *Travel Writing 1700–1830: An Anthology* (Oxford: Oxford University Press, 2005).

Ian Brown, 'Myth, Political Caricature and Monstering the Tartan', in Ian Brown (ed.), *From Tartan to Tartanry: Scottish Culture, History and Myth* (Edinburgh: Edinburgh University Press, 2010), pp. 93–114.

David Bruce, *Scotland the Movie* (Edinburgh: Polygon, 1996).

John Buchan, *The Thirty Nine Steps*, in *The Complete Richard Hannay* (London: Penguin, 1956).

John Buchanan, *A Defence of the Scots Highlanders* (London: Edgerton, 1794).

Charles Burlington, David Llewellyn Rees and Alexander Murray, *The Modern Universal British Traveller; or, a New, Complete, and Accurate Tour through England, Wales, Scotland, and the Neighbouring Islands. Comprising all that is Worthy of Observation in Great Britain* (London: J. Cooke, 1779).

Robert Burns *The Letters of Robert Burns*, ed. G. Ross Roy (Oxford: Oxford University Press, 1985).

Richard Butt, 'Literature and the Screen Media since 1908', in Ian Brown *et al.* (eds.), *The Edinburgh History of Scottish Literature* (Edinburgh: Edinburgh University Press, 2007), vol. 3, pp. 53–63.

Richard Butt, 'Looking at the Tartan in Film: History, Identity and Spectacle', in Ian Brown (ed.), *From Tartan to Tartanry: Scottish Culture, History and Myth* (Edinburgh: Edinburgh University Press, 2010), pp. 165–179.

Michel Byrne, 'Mairearad Ghriogarach: Sùil Thòiseachail air Bana-Bhard air Dìochuimhne', *Scottish Gaelic Studies*, 23 (2007), pp. 85–122.

Thomas Owen Clancy (ed.), *The Triumph Tree: Scotland's Earliest Poetry AD 550–1350* (Edinburgh: Canongate, 1998).

Robert Clyde, *From Rebel to Hero: the Image of the Highlander 1745–1830* (East Linton: Tuckwell, 1995).

Lord [Henry] Cockburn, *Life of Francis Jeffrey* (Edinburgh: Adam and Charles Black, new edition, 1874).

Henry Cockburn, *Circuit Journeys* (Edinburgh: David Douglas, 1888).

Lord [Henry] Cockburn, *Circuit Journeys,* (Hawick: Byways, 1983).

A. O. J. Cockshut, *The Achievement of Walter Scott* (London: Collins, 1969).

Samuel Coleridge, *Scottish Notes.*

Samuel Coleridge, *Collected Letters of Samuel Taylor Coleridge, volume III, 1807–1814,* ed. E. L. Griggs (Oxford: Oxford University Press, 1959).

Charles Cordiner, *Antiquities of the North of Scotland in a Series of Letters to Thomas Pennant* (London: independently published, 1780).

Cairns Craig, 'Myths against History: Tartanry and Kailyard in 19th-Century Scottish Literature' in Colin McArthur (ed.), *Scotch Reels* (London: British Film Institute, 1982).

Thomas John Dibdin, *The lady of the lake; a melo-dramatic romance in two acts (from Sir Walter Scott) printed from the Acting Copy [...]* (London, [1810]).

Mrs Diggle, *Journal of a tour from London to the Highlands of Scotland,* 19 April to 7 August 1788, Letter 23rd, Gretna. Glasgow University Library, Special Collections MS Gen. 738.

Alastair J. Durie, 'Unconscious Benefactors: Grouse-shooting in Scotland', *International Journal of the History of Sport* (December 1998), pp. 57–73.

Alastair J. Durie, *Scotland for the Holidays: Tourism in Scotland c. 1780–1939* (East Linton: Tuckwell, 2003).

Edmund John Eyre, *The Lady of the Lake: A Melodramatic Romance in three acts; taken from the popular poem of that title, and now performing with undiminished applause at the Theatre Royal, Edinburgh* (London, 1811).

William Fergusson, *The Identity of the Scottish Nation: An Historic Quest* (Edinburgh: Edinburgh University Press, 1998).

Gerald Finley, *Landscapes of Memory: Turner as illustrator to Scott* (London: Scolar, 1980).

Theodore Fontane, *Across the Tweed: A Tour of Mid-Victorian Scotland,* tr. Brian Battershaw, intro. Sir James Fergusson (London: Phoenix House, 1965).

Theodor Fontane, *Beyond the Tweed: a tour of Scotland in 1858* (German original, *Jenseit des Tweed,* 1860; English translation, London: Libris, 1998).

Tom Furniss, '"Plumb-Pudding Stone" and the Romantic Sublime: The Landscape and Geology of the Trossachs in *The Statistical Account of Scotland* (1791–99)', in Christoph Bode and Jacqueline Labbe (eds.), *Romantic Localities: Europe Writes Place* (London: Pickering and Chatto: 2010), pp. 51–65.

Thomas Garnett, *Observations on a Tour through the Highlands and Part of the Western Isles of Scotland* (London, 1800).

A. A. Gill, 'Rupert Penry-Jones Shines in The Thirty-Nine Steps', *The Sunday Times,* 4 January 2009.

Upcott Gill, *Guide to the Inland Watering Places of Great Britain and Ireland* (London: Upcott Gill, 1891).

William Gillies, 'On the Study of Gaelic Literature', in Michel Byrne, Thomas Owen Clancy & Sheila Kidd (eds.) *Litreachas & Eachdraidh: Rannsachadh na Gàidhlig 2, Glaschu 2002 / Literature & History: Papers from the Second Conference of Scottish Gaelic Studies, Glasgow 2002* (Glasgow: University of Glasgow, 2006), pp. 1–32.

John Glendenning, *The High Road: Romantic Tourism, Scotland, and Literature 1720–1820* (Basingstoke: Palgrave Macmillan, 1997).

Francis Grose, *The Antiquities of Scotland* (London: Hooper & Wigstead, 1797).

John and Margaret Gold, *Imagining Scotland: Tradition, Representation and Promotion in Scottish Tourism since 1750* (Aldershot: Scolar, 1995).

Patrick Graham, *Sketches descriptive of picturesque scenery on the southern confines of Perthshire including The Trosachs and that district of the country in which the scene of the "Lady of the Lake" is laid. With notices of natural history* (Edinburgh: Peter Hill, 1806).

Mrs Grant of Laggan, *Memoir and Correspondence of Mrs Grant of Laggan*, edited by her son, J. P. Grant (London: Longman, Brown, Green and Longmans, 1844).

Katherine Haldane Grenier, *Tourism and Identity in Scotland 1770–1914* (Aldershot: Scolar, 2005).

H. J. C. Grierson (ed.), *The Letters of Sir Walter Scott, 1808–1811* (London: Constable, 1932).

F. H. Groome (ed.), *Ordnance Gazetteer of Scotland*, (Edinburgh: T. C. Jack, 1882–1885).

H. J. C. Grierson, *Letters of Sir Walter Scott: 1808–1811* (London: Constable, 1932).

Betty Hagglund, *Tourists and Travellers: Women's Non-Fictional Writing About Scotland, 1770–1830* (Bristol: Channel View, 2010).

Forsyth Hardy, *Scotland in Film* (Edinburgh: Edinburgh University Press, 1990).

Robert Heron *Scotland Delineated, or a Geographical Description of every Shire in Scotland, Including the Northern and Western Isles. With some Account of the Curiosities, Antiquities, and Present State of the Country. For the use of Young Persons* (Edinburgh: James Neill, 1791).

David Hewitt, '*Rob Roy* and First Person Narratives', in *Scott and His Influence*, ed. J. H. Alexander and David Hewitt (Aberdeen: Association for Scottish Literary Studies, 1983), pp. 372–81.

Christopher Hibbert, *Queen Victoria: a Personal History* (London: Harper Collins, 2000).

Tim Hilton, *John Ruskin: the Early Years* (New Haven and London: Yale University Press, 2000).

James Hogg, 'Highland Adventures', in *Winter Evening Tales, collected among the cottagers in the south of Scotland*, 2nd edn. (Edinburgh: Oliver and Boyd, 1821), 2 vols.

James Hogg, *James Hogg's Highland Tours*, ed. W. F. Lauchlan (Hawick: Byway Books, 1981).

James Holloway and Lindsay Errington, *The Discovery of Scotland: The Appreciation of Scottish Scenery through Two Centuries of Painting* (Edinburgh: National Gallery of Scotland, 1978).

Gerard Manley Hopkins, *Poems*, ed. R. Bridges (London: Humphrey Milford, 1918).

Washington Irving, *Abbotsford and Newstead Abbey* (London: John Murray, 1835).

Edgar Johnson, *Sir Walter Scott: the Great Unknown* (London: Hamilton, 1970), 2 vols.

Louise Jury, 'Location, Location, Location: A Movie Buff's Choice', *The Independent*, 23 July 2005

Stuart Kelly, *Scott-land: The Man Who Invented A Nation* (Edinburgh: Polygon, 2010)·

James M'Nair, *A Guide from Glasgow to Some of the Most Remarkable Scenes in the Highlands of Scotland and to the Falls of Clyde* (Glasgow: Courier Office, 1797).

Robert Kirk, *The Secret Common-Wealth an Essay of the Nature and actions of the Subterranean and (for the most part) Invisible people heiretoforgoing under the names of ELVES, FAUNES and FAIRIES* [...] in Michael Hunter, *The Occult Laboratory* (Woodbridge; Boydell Press, 2001).

Kristin Lach-Szyrma, *From Charlotte Square to Fingal's Cave: Reminiscences of a Journey through Scotland, 1820–1824*, ed. M. K. Mcleod (East Linton: Tuckwell Press, 2004).

Bruce Lenman, *The Jacobite Risings in Britain 1689–1746* (London: Methuen, 1980).

John Leyden, *Journal of a Tour in the Highlands and Western Islands of Scotland in 1800*, ed. James Sinton (Edinburgh and London: Blackwood, 1903).

John Gibson Lockhart, *Memoirs of the Life of Sir Walter Scott, Bart.* (Edinburgh: Robert Cadell, 1837–38), 7 vols.

John Gibson Lockhart. *Memoirs of Sir Walter Scott* (London: Macmillan, 1900), 5 vols.

John Gibson Lockhart, *The Life of Sir Walter Scott*, Edinburgh Edition (Edinburgh: T. C. Jack and E. C. Jack, 1902), 10 vols.

Allison Lockwood, *Passionate Pilgrims: The American Traveler in Great Britain, 1800–1914* (New York and London: Cornwall Books, 1981).

Dr Lucas, *Diary of Dr Lucas*, Stirling Archives, PD 16/4/2.

John MacCulloch, *The Highlands and Western Islands of Scotland, Containing Descriptions of their Scenery and Antiquities [...] Founded as a Series of Annual Journeys between the years 1811 and 1821, and forming a universal guide to that country, in Letters to Sir Walter Scott, Bart.* (London: Longman *et al.*, 1824), 4 vols.

Murdo Macdonald, 'The Visual Preconditions of Celtic Revival Art in Scotland', *Journal of the Scottish Society for Art History*, vol. 13, 'Highlands' issue (2008–2009), pp. 16–21.

T. McDonald and E. Tomlinson, 'Little Suite: March – Trevor Duncan (b.1924)', CD sleeve note, *Elizabethan Serenade: The Best of British Light Music* (Munich: MVD Music, 1996).

Gregor MacGregor (ed.), *Ceileairean Binn nan Creagan Aosda* (Glasgow: D. McKenzie, 1819).

Ray McKenzie, *Public Sculpture of Glasgow* (Liverpool: Liverpool University Press, 2002).

Donald MacLeod, *Memoir of Norman MacLeod, D.D.* (London, 1877).

Charles Macready, *Macready's reminiscences, and Selections from his Diaries and Letters*, ed. Sir Frederick Pollock (London, 1875), 2 vols.

Donald Mason, 'James Stuart of Killin', *Highland Monthly*, 1 (1889), pp. 494–9.

Donald Meek, 'The pulpit and the pen: clergy, orality and print in the Scottish Gaelic world', in Adam Fox and Daniel Woolf (eds.), *The Spoken Word: Oral Culture in Britain, 1500–1850* (Manchester: Manchester University Press, 2002), pp. 84–118.

Donald Meek, 'The Sublime Gael: The Impact of Macpherson's "Ossian" on Literary Creativity and Cultural Perception in Gaelic Scotland', in Howard Gaskill (ed.), *The Reception of Ossian in Europe* (London: Thommes, 2004), pp. 40–66.

Martin Meisel, *Realizations: Narrative, Pictorial, and Theatrical Arts in Nineteenth-century England* (Princeton: Princeton University Press, 1983).

Karl Miller, *Cockburn's Millennium* (London: Duckworth, 1975).

Mary Moorman, *William Wordsworth: A Biography; the Later Years, 1803–1850* (Oxford: Clarendon Press, 1965).

John Muir, *John Muir Correspondence,* Holt-Atherton Special Collections, University of the Pacific, Stockton, California.

Sarah Murray, *A Companion, and Useful Guide to the Beauties of Scotland, to the Lakes of Westmoreland, Cumberland, and Lancashire; and to the Curiosities in the District of Craven, in the West Riding of Yorkshire. To which is added, a more particular Description of Scotland, especially that part of it, called the Highlands. By the Hon. Mrs Murray, of Kensington* (London: G. Nicol, 1799).

Sarah Murray, *A Companion and Useful Guide to the Beauties of Scotland,* first published in 1799, ed. W. F. Laughlan (Hawick: Byway Books, 1982).

Stana Nenadic, ' Land, the landed and relationships with England: literature and perception 1760–1830', in S. Connolly, R. Houston and R. J. Morris (eds.), *Conflict, Identity and Economic Development* (Preston: Carnegie, 1995), pp. 148–160.

Michael Newton (ed.), *Bho Chluaidh gu Calasraid / From the Clyde to Callander* (Stornoway: Acair, 1999).

Michael Newton, 'Early Poetry in the MacGregor Papers', *Scottish Gaelic Studies,* 21 (2003), pp. 47–58.

Kristin Ott, 'Sublime Landscapes and Ancient Traditions: Eighteenth-Century Literary Tourism in Scotland', in Christoph Bode and Jacqueline Labbe (eds.), *Romantic Localities: Europe Writes Place* (London: Pickering and Chatto: 2010), pp. 39–50.

Samuel Pegge, *Anecdotes of the English Language* (London, 1800).

Duncan Petrie, *Screening Scotland* (London: British Film Institute, 2000).

Joseph Jean M. C. Amédée Pichot, *Historical and Literary Tour of a Foreigner in England and Scotland* (London: Saunders and Ottley, 1825), 2 vols.

Isaac Pocock, *Rob Roy or Auld Langsyne, an Operatic Drama in Three Acts* (London: John Miller, 1818).

A. J. J. Ratcliffe, *Scott's Narrative Poetry, Being Abridgements of The Lay of the Last Minstrel, Marmion, and The Lady of the Lake* (London and Edinburgh: Nelson, 1927).

Arthur R. B. Robinson, *Seeking the Scots: An English Woman's Journey in 1807* (Skelton: A.R.B. Robinson, 2006).

Thomas Pennant, *A Tour in Scotland, 1769*, intr. Brian D. Osborne (Edinburgh: Birlinn, 2000 [1771]).

Thomas Pennant, *A Tour in Scotland and Voyage to the Hebrides, 1772* in 2 vols, ed. Andrew Simmons (Edinburgh: Birlinn, 1998 [1774, 1776]).

Reverend James Robertson, 'Parish of Callander', in Sir John Sinclair (ed.), *The Statistical Account of Scotland, Drawn up from the Communications of the Ministers of the Different Parishes* in 21 vols. (Edinburgh: William Creech, 1791–1799), vol. XI, pp.574–627. [The Old Statistical Account is also available as an online version produced by EDINA at the University of Edinburgh].

Charles Roger, *A Week at Bridge of Allan comprising an account of the Airthrey Spa and a series of six excursions to the interesting scenery around this rising watering place* (Edinburgh: Lizars 1853, reprinted Heritage Press, 1980).

Charles Ross, *The Traveller's Guide to Lochlomond, and its Environs. Illustrated with a Map* (Paisley, 1792).

Norman Scarfe, *To The Highlands in 1786: The Inquisitive Journey of a Young French Aristocrat* (Woodbridge: Boydell Press, 2001).

Walter Scott, *Rob Roy*, ed. Ian Duncan (Oxford: Oxford University Press, 1998).

Walter Scott, *Rob Roy*, ed. David Hewitt, Edinburgh Edition of the Waverley Novels, vol. 5 (Edinburgh: Edinburgh University Press, 2008).

Walter Scott, *Waverley*, ed. P. D. Garside (Edinburgh: Edinburgh University Press, 2007).

Walter Scott, *The Lady of the Lake. A Poem by Walter Scott Esq. Illustrated with engravings from paintings by Richard Cook/with engravings from the designs of Richard Westall* (Edinburgh, 1811; London: John Sharpe, 1811).

Walter Scott, *The Lady of the Lake*, in *The Poetical Works of Sir Walter Scott, Bart.* [ed. J. G. Lockhart] (Edinburgh: Robert Cadell, 1833–34), 12 vols.

Walter Scott, *The Lady of the Lake*, (Edinburgh: Ballantyne 1810); new edition, Thomas Crawford (ed.), (Glasgow: Association for Scottish Literary Studies, 2010).

Walter Scott, *The Waverley Novels*, 48 vols. (Edinburgh: Robert Cadell, 1829–33).

Louis Simond, *Journal of a Tour and Residence in Great Britain, during the years 1810 and 1811* (2nd ed. Edinburgh: Constable, 1817 [1815]), 2 vols.

Katharine Simms, 'Muireadhach Albanach Ó Dálaigh and the Classical Revolution', in Ian Brown *et al.* (ed.) *The Edinburgh History of Scottish Literature* (Edinburgh: Edinburgh University Press, 2007) vol. 2, pp. 83–90.

T. C. Smout, 'Tours in the Scottish Highlands from the Eighteenth to the Twentieth Century', *Northern Scotland*, 5.2 (1983), pp. 99–121.

Elizabeth Isabella Spence, *Sketches of the manners, customs and scenery of Scotland* (London: Longmans, 1811).

David Stevenson, *The Hunt for Rob Roy: the Man and the Myths* (Edinburgh: John Donald, 2004).

John Stoddart, *Remarks on Local Scenery and Manners in Scotland during the Years 1799 and 1800*, (London: W. Miller, 1801), 2 vols.

Louis Stott, *Ring of Words: The Trossachs* (Milton of Aberfoyle: Creag Darach Publications, 1997).

Bayard Taylor, *Views a-foot, or, Europe seen with knapsack and staff* (New York: G.P. Putnam, 1859).

Kathleen Tillotson, 'Charlotte Yonge as a Critic of literature', in Georgina Battiscombe and Marghanita Laski (eds.), *A Chaplet for Charlotte Yonge* (London: Cresset Press, 1965).

Carol Kyros Walker *Breaking Away: Coleridge in Scotland* (New Haven and London: Yale University Press, 2002).

Nicola J. Watson, *The Literary Tourist: Readers and Places in Romantic and Victorian Britain* (Basingstoke: Palgrave Macmillan, 2006).

Nicola J. Watson, 'Readers of Romantic Locality: Tourists, Loch Katrine and *The Lady of the Lake*', in Christoph Bode and Jacqueline Labbe (eds.), *Romantic Localities: Europe Writes Place* (London: Pickering and Chatto, 2010), pp. 67–79.

William J. Watson (ed.) *Bàrdachd Albannach O Leabhar Deadhan Lios-Mòir / Scottish Verse from the Book of the Dean of Lismore* (Scottish Gaelic Texts 1), (Edinburgh: Scottish Gaelic Texts Society, 1937).

[John Wilkes], *The North Briton*, No. 46 (Saturday, May 28, 1763).

N. T. Willis, *Abbotsford* (London, 1854).

William Wilson, *The Trossachs in Literature and Tradition* (Stirling, 1908).

Andrew Wilton, *J. M. W. Turner: His Art and Life* (New York: Rizzoli International Publications, 1979).

Lynne Withey, *Grand Tours and Cook's Tours* (New York: Morrow, 1997).

D. J. Withrington and I.R. Grant *et al.* (eds.), *The Statistical Account of Scotland* (Wakefield: EP Publishing, 1973–1983), 20 vols.

Gillen d'Arcy Wood, 'Working Holiday: Turner as Waverley Tourist', *The Wordsworth Circle* 31: 2 (Spring 2000), pp. 83–88.

Dorothy Wordsworth, *Recollections of a Tour Made in Scotland, AD 1803*, ed. John Campbell Shairp (New York, 1874).

Dorothy Wordsworth, *Recollections of a Tour Made in Scotland in 1803* in *The Journals of Dorothy Wordsworth*, ed. Ernest de Selincourt (London, 1941), 2 vols.

Dorothy Wordsworth, *Recollections of a Tour Made in Scotland, AD 1803*, ed. Carol Kyros Walker (New Haven and London: Yale University Press, 1997).

Duncan Wu, *Wordsworth's Reading, 1800–1815* (Cambridge and New York: Cambridge University Press, 1995).

Jules Verne, *The Underground City* (French original, *Les Indes noires*, 1877: English translation, Edinburgh: Luath Press, 2005).

Arthur Young, *A Six Months Tour Through the North of England* (London, Salisbury, and Edinburgh: W. Strahan, 1770), 4 vols.

Notes on contributors

Jim Alison, a retired HM Inspector of Schools and former secretary of the Association for Scottish Literary Studies, helped to plan the 2010 ASLS conference on *Sir Walter Scott, the Trossachs and the Tourists*. He has edited an anthology of the poetry of north-east Scotland and has made a study of Scottish children's books.

Ian Brown is playwright, poet and Professor in Drama and Dance at Kingston University. General Editor of *The Edinburgh History of Scottish Literature* (2007), he has most recently edited *From Tartan to Tartanry: Scottish Culture, History and Myth* (2010) and *The Edinburgh Companion to Scottish Drama* (2011). ASLS President and Chair of the Scottish Society of Playwrights, he is visiting professor at Glasgow and Glamorgan Universities and publishes on theatrical, literary and cultural topics.

Alastair Durie has had a long career as teacher, researcher, writer and reviewer, first at Aberdeen, then Glasgow and latterly Stirling, and for the Open University. His publications originally centred in mainstream Scottish economic history, but recently focus on the development of tourism in Scotland. A particular interest has been health tourism, and *Water is Best* (2006) discussed that very Scottish institution, the hydro. *Scotland for the Holidays* (2003) took the story of tourism in Scotland up to 1939. He is currently working on its sequel, provisionally entitled *Scotland no more for holidays*.

Tom Furniss is Senior Lecturer in English Studies at the University of Strathclyde in Glasgow. He is the author of *Edmund Burke's Aesthetic Ideology* (1993) and *Reading Poetry* (2007), together with a number of articles on the politics and philosophy of the late Enlightenment. His developing interest in the Romantic writing of Scottish landscape is reflected in recent essays on the landscape and geology of the Trossachs and on James Hutton's 1788 'Theory of the Earth'.

David Hewitt is editor-in-chief of the Edinburgh Edition of the Waverley Novels. Before his retirement in 2008, he was Regius Chalmers Professor of English at the University of Aberdeen. He is an Honorary Fellow of the Association for Scottish Literary Studies.

Murdo Macdonald is Professor of History of Scottish Art at the University of Dundee. He is a former editor of *Edinburgh Review*. He is author of *Scottish Art* (2000) in Thames and Hudson's 'World of Art' series. His recent research has explored the art of the Highland Gàidhealtachd; Robert Burns and visual thinking; and the cultural milieu of Patrick Geddes. He is an honorary member of the Royal Scottish Academy.

Dorothy McMillan is Honorary Senior Research Fellow in English Literature at the University of Glasgow. She has published widely on women's writing. Formerly Secretary, then President of Association for Scottish Literary Studies, she is now an Honorary Fellow of the Association.

David Manderson lectures in Creative Writing and Screenwriting at the University of the West of Scotland. He has written two *Scotnotes* study guides on Scottish films, and a novel, *Lost Bodies*, a chilling psychological thriller (2011), published by Kennedy and Boyd. He runs the regular Reading Allowed live performance events at the Tchai Ovna Teahouse in Glasgow's West End.

Michael Newton is an Assistant Professor in the Celtic Studies department of St Francis Xavier University, Nova Scotia. He has written several books and numerous articles on many aspects of Highland tradition and history in Scotland and North America. He edited *Dùthchas nan Gaidheal: Selected Essays of John MacInnes*, which won the Saltire Society's Research Book award of 2006, and is author of *Warriors of the Word: The World of the Scottish Highlanders*, nominated for the 2009 Katharine Briggs Award for folklore research.

Ian Thompson is Emeritus Professor of Geography at the University of Glasgow. He has conducted research on the travels of Jules Verne in Malta and Gibraltar, but more particularly on his journeys in Scotland and the novels that resulted from this experience. Author of numerous articles on

Verne, his Scottish research was published in *Jules Verne's Scotland, in fact and fiction* (2011). He has written essays to accompany new translations of *The Underground City* (2005), *The Green Ray* (2009) and *The Blockade Runners* (2011), all published by Luath Press.

Nicola Watson currently works for the Open University. Her research on the reception and adaptation of literary figures and texts ranges across the late eighteenth and nineteenth centuries. An interest in Walter Scott threads throughout her diverse publications, including *Revolution and the Form of the British Novel, 1790–1825* (1994) and *The Literary Tourist: Readers and Places in Romantic and Victorian Britain* (2006). She has edited Scott's *The Antiquary* (for OUP, 2002) and two collections, including *Literary Tourism and Nineteenth-century Culture* (2009).